CREATIVE IDEAS FOR
SACRAMENTAL WORSHIP WITH CHILDREN

Creative Ideas for Sacramental Worship with Children

Simon Rundell

CANTERBURY
PRESS
Norwich

© Simon Rundell

Published in 2011 by Canterbury Press
Editorial office
13–17 Long Lane,
London EC1A 9PN, UK

Canterbury Press is an imprint of Hymns Ancient & Modern Ltd
(a registered charity)
13A Hellesdon Park Road,
Norwich NR6 5DR

www.canterburypress.co.uk

British Library Cataloguing in Publication data

A catalogue record for this book is available
from the British Library

978 1 84825 092 5

Typeset by Regent Typesetting, London
Printed and bound by
CPI Antony Rowe, Chippenham, Wiltshire

Contents

Acknowledgements

No book is ever really the work of one single person, and a book on worship and liturgy is supported, shaped and influenced by the whole community from which it derives. Much of this work springs from the Parish of St Thomas the Apostle, Elson (http://www.saintthomaselson.org.uk): a distinctly family-orientated, child-friendly inclusive Anglo-Catholic community in Gosport in the Anglican Diocese of Portsmouth and the uniquely sacramental alternative worship community which finds its home there: Blesséd (http://www.blessed.org.uk). I want to especially thank my extra-special friends Steven Smart and Vickie Williams for their ideas, prayer, advice and reflection. Lorraine Rundell, my lovely wife, who diligently prepares dozens of children for Admission to Holy Communion will always be my muse and the source of all kinds of great ideas: thank you.

I would like to give special thanks and credit to my daughter, Emma Rundell, whose creativity with animation and illustration has done such a lot to shape the visual style of Blesséd's expression of the liturgy of the word. I love her simple, amusing and yet profound illustrations, and I thank her for letting me use so many of them here.

Thanks are also due to Fr John Draper, Fr Paul Robinson and Fr Bob Cooper for their insights, materials and ideas. A number of the examples in this book have clearly been influenced by the genius of Johnny Baker and Mthr Sue Wallace. I am sure their influence is felt in the DNA of so many other writers and liturgists these days.

If there are errors, either practical or theological, these are my fault. Everything written in this book, however, is done in a spirit of playful enquiry and a desire to worship almighty God in spirit and truth. I recognize that sometimes this doesn't always sit well with the establishment and the polite society that is so often associated with the Church, and yet I feel sure that God wants us to be creative, to be playful in worship and share his holy sacraments with the whole world.

1

Introduction

'Children are the Church of tomorrow.'

I've heard that said so many times, and I always think, 'What rubbish! Children are the Church of *today*.' Just as you and I are the Church of today, we are the body of Christ, his Church, of the present. Each and every person has a valid part to play in the worship of almighty God, regardless of their age, gender, colour or anything else for that matter.[1] Just as the body of Christ is reflected by the diversity of the Church, so the worship of the Church must, by necessity, be a full expression of all those who come to worship.

Children have special needs, and yet these special needs should not mean that they are excluded from the worshipping life of the Church, given a watered-down or inauthentic experience of worship just because they are young.[2]

This book is concerned with sacramental worship with children: not *for* children, for that denies their engagement, neither is it *to* children, for they are not passive recipients; but we will be discussing worship *with* children, which implies engagement, involvement and participation.

The parish church in which I serve as priest,[3] and the alternative worship community that makes its home there,[4] have both discovered that with the full participation of children in the life of the parish the whole life and witness of the church is enriched. It is true to say that the involvement of children in the sacramental life has revitalized us, given us all new insights into the journey of faith that we are all on, and provided us with rich opportunities to rediscover what Christ really meant when he called the children to gather around him.[5]

---

1 Acts 2.17–21.

2 H. Thomas (2010), 'Suffer Little Children – Don't Fob Them Off', *Church Times*, 22 October 2010, p. 14.

3 http://www.saintthomaselson.org.uk.

4 http://www.blessed.org.uk.

5 Luke 18.16.

The good news is that each and every parish can involve the children in their midst in meaningful and authentic sacramental worship: local schools (and especially those associated with faith) are crying out for a meaningful connection with their local faith community, and you can offer to young people throughout your locality something which is both sincere to our time-honoured Christian heritage and profoundly missional and attractive. This book seeks to provide you with some resources to reach out and draw young people into the sacramental life, and to show that there is something even more alive beyond Xbox Live.

Involving Children

I firmly believe that children can and should be involved in the planning, contribution and ministry of all kinds of worship and that this should include the sacramental forms of worship. Although the order of the Church limits certain sacramental acts to those set apart ('ordained') for some forms of ministry, this does not preclude the involvement of the young in support of those sacramental acts which are the life-blood of the Church which proclaims Jesus Christ as Lord.

In the Gospel of Matthew[6] Jesus calls Andrew, Peter, James and John from their fishing boats. The text specifically notes that James and John were working with their father, which implies that, having failed the educational demands of Rabinnical School (as did Jesus, it is believed), they were apprenticed to their father to learn their trade, and hadn't yet completed this in order to set up on their own. This would imply that at the time Jesus called them, they may have been as young as 14 or 15.

Yet Jesus calls them.

So often we disregard the action of the Holy Spirit in the young and expect them to be passive recipients of faith rather than spiritual beings in themselves.

Peter and Penny Go Swimming

Soon after Peter and Penny were born, their parents began taking them to the local swimming pool every weekend. The parents were enthusiastic swimmers, and they hoped their children would be keen swimmers too.

---

6 Matthew 4.21.

Of course Peter and Penny were not allowed to go the swimming pool itself, they were looked after in a little room right beside the pool. Sometimes they cried because they wanted to stay with their parents, but that wasn't allowed because they might disturb the adult swimmers. Besides, they were too young to understand swimming, and they wouldn't appreciate it fully.

When Peter and Penny were three years old, they were allowed to go to another room just down the hall from the swimming pool. There they heard stories from the *Swimmer's Manual*, and they coloured pictures of people swimming.

When they were six years old, Peter and Penny went to another big room – a big room with lots of children. Here they began to get really serious about swimming. For the first ten or fifteen minutes they were allowed to take off their shoes and socks and splash around in the wading pool. They then went to classes with other children their own age to learn more about swimming. They were taught by some dedicated people who loved swimming, but who hardly ever swam themselves any more because they were busy with the children.

By the time Peter and Penny were thirteen, they had studied the *Swimmer's Manual* in even more detail and had learned the rules of the swimming pool by heart: 'You will not run on the deck, you shall not bring flotation devices into the pool area ...' They had also learned about the properties of water, the muscles used in swimming, and the various swimming strokes. They had studied great swimmers of the past, including Olympic medal winners.

They had heard about swimmers who went to other countries such as Africa or India to teach swimming, and they had seen slides of groups of African or Indian swimmers standing beside their swimming pools. On special occasions, Peter and Penny had been allowed to go with their parents into the pool as long as they didn't splash around too much and disturb the other swimmers or bother the life-guard.

At last Peter and Penny finished swimming school and were allowed to accompany their parents into the swimming pool every week. They tried it a few times. Much to the disappointment of their parents, Peter and Penny had lost interest and preferred to watch television instead.[7]

This is, I believe a salutary lesson for us all, regardless of the style of church God calls us to. Involvement and engagement go far beyond the giving of a candle for them to hold.

That full engagement with worship can be systematically denied to children throughout the Church should be a source of shame to us all. We have, at times,

7 Janet Marshall Eibner and Susan Graham Walker (1997), *God, Kids and Us*. Harrisburg, PA: Morehouse Publishing, pp. 49–50.

failed to see children as valid members of the body of Christ and have swapped the experience of faith for religion as yet another curriculum subject: to be taught rather than felt.

Children have great capacity to relate to the sign and symbol of sacramental worship often beyond that of cynical confirming adults (who choose to reject symbolism because 'that's not how we do it in this church'). They are immersed in symbolic language, in creative imagery and metaphor in school, in their books and on television. For these reasons they are no stranger to the symbolic language and the semiotics of faith. Glance at any primary school library shelf and wonder at the variety, complexity and beauty of children's literature. Then compare that to the stilted prose and unimaginative recounts that pass for many modern bestselling adult books. No wonder that modern cross-over successes like J. K. Rowling's *Harry Potter* series, the Philip Pullman *His Dark Materials* books or the C. S. Lewis *Narnia Chronicles* are so popular with adults.

Jesus himself rarely spoke directly of God but instead used parables and tangible objects (spittle, dust, bread and wine) to make real the kingdom of God and open out to us the wonderful opportunities of eternal life. In what Jesus taught us there is imagination, flair and imagery which would have made our Lord the best children's (and adults' come to think of it) writer of all time.

The story of Scripture is also sacramental: visceral realities, sign and symbol to explore the unimaginable wonder of God. I want to assert that all churches act sacramentally, even though they might – through theology, ecclesiology or history – want to deny that: to exist as the body of Christ is to enter into a sacramental engagement with the God which is both engaged with this world in the form of Jesus Christ and beyond all understanding.[8]

With this understanding, it soon becomes nonsensical to place barriers between children and the sacraments, beyond making them passive recipients of baptism. I want therefore to introduce to you a reinterpretation of the sacramental life which is grounded in the deep tradition of the Church, which draws upon the heritage which we know and love, but which seeks to proclaim that Good News afresh for these generations: taking what is well established and seeking to connect it with younger people, without trivialization or being patronizing.

You already have the tools for this to hand: broken bread and wine outpoured; oil and water; hands to be laid on and blessings to be pronounced. I would like to instil in all those who encounter this book the confidence to go out there and share the sacraments with confidence and vigour with the young people in your midst.

---

8 S. Rundell (2010), *Creative Ideas for Alternative Sacramental Worship*. Norwich: Canterbury Press, pp. 4–5.

The Shape of This Book

The next chapter gives an overview of the spirituality of young people which will ask how the sacramental life can be used as a tool of engagement and a powerful missionary tool.

In Chapter 3, I will return to the role of storytelling in the sacramental life and explore ways in which we can draw on the Christian faith's greatest asset: a body of stories which has the power to captivate, challenge and transform all generations, but most effectively children.

The final chapter contains a variety of liturgies and ideas which can be incorporated into your own sacramental encounters: some are complete liturgies, some are fragments or ideas from which your own creativity can flow.

In the Church of England, children may be admitted to Holy Communion, and the *ad hoc* practice of individual parishes was codified in 2006.[9] It is interesting to note that it remains firmly within the permission of the local bishop and shaped by the incumbent of the parish. I am pleased to note that although the involvement of children in the sacramental life raises few outright objections, there is sometimes a sense of shuffling embarrassment which quietly blocks their full participation in this most fundamental of Christian worship. This may be because many Christian communities have few children, and fail to communicate the incredible possibilities of a life drenched in the sacraments, or that we are scared to cross traditional boundaries. Other churches have different practices which range from the formal first communion of the Roman Catholic Church through to a decision made in a church at a local level.

Throughout this book I will use the phrase 'young people' interchangeably with 'children', although I prefer the former as it carries more dignity for the person we are talking about. To be a child carries cultural and scriptural baggage which, I find, personally challenges me; but my wife, who is a teacher, tells me not to be so silly.

---

9 Church of England Admission of Baptised Children to Holy Communion Regulations 2006, http://www.cofe.anglican.org/info/education/children/childrencommunion.doc, accessed 22 May 2011.

2

The Spirituality of Young People

The greatest sin of the Church is to have sidelined and disregarded the spirituality of children. In the culture of the first century, children (and women) were merely assets of male ownership,[10] and this is what Jesus spoke against when he embraced and blessed the children in his midst. In my reading of Scripture, Christ shows that children have value far beyond their monetary one, and the assurance of a place in heaven.[11] As most of Christ's teaching was concerned with our relationship with God, and the eternal reward that is the result of that intimate relationship, I am struck by the affinity of children for matters spiritual and their lack of *a priori* assumptions which enables them to engage with faith in all its varied glory, which includes formal religion. When Jesus calls adults to be like children to enter the kingdom of heaven, it would seem to imply that the innate openness of children brings them to that place ahead of us, despite our attempts to sideline or diminish young people in church.

The 1988 Education Act stated that as well as moral, cultural, mental and physical development, the education system should 'promote the spiritual development of pupils in school and society'.[12] Nye noted that 'It became clear that this was a generic task, not restricted to the provision made by religious education. This required a broader, more open, examination of what "spiritual" might mean.'[13] She further remarks that this meant that the interest in Britain

---

10 Leviticus 27.6.

11 'I tell you the truth, unless you change and become like little children, you will never enter the kingdom of heaven' (Matthew 18.3).

12 DES (1989), *The Education Reform Act 1988: School Curriculum and Assessment.* London: HMSO, p. 7.

13 R. Nye (2009), 'Spirituality', in A. Richards and P. Privitt (eds), *Through the Eyes of a Child: New Insights in Theology from a Child's Perspective.* London: Church House Publishing, p. 70.

in children's spirituality came largely from educationalists rather than from the churches, and it would seem to suggest that the agenda has been seized by them away from the Church. If one was to witness a typical act of Collective Worship[14] in a non-church school, then you would usually encounter a generic reflection on humanity rather than an exploration of any facet of organized religion, and certainly not worship which was 'broadly Christian' in the words of the 1944 Education Act.

However, if the purpose is to explore and expand the spiritual element which is inside all of us, then this cannot be criticized. Although the Church appears to have abrogated its responsibility in most non-denominational settings, this form of generic faith Collective Worship can be used as a foundation for more focused evangelization outside of the school curriculum and back within the Church's domain: in the youth clubs, the Sunday schools and the parks and street corners, which is where we should rightly be working with most young people.

In recent years there have been a number of interesting ideas in the development of a theology of children's spirituality and a move away from the idea that children were incomplete until they had learned and internalized the prayers, practices and beliefs of tradition. Of perhaps the greatest interest is the innovation of Godly Play[15] which uses the wonder of storytelling and an open-question style of engagement with children.

Even more challenging is the wealth of literature and thinking that has exploded on children's spirituality; this has largely focused upon the non-sacramental: perhaps as a result of the current ascendency of evangelicalism, while ignoring the notion that children act and respond to the world in a sacramental way – their capacity for awe and wonder and their openness to sign and symbol would seem to suggest that one of the best ways to explore matters of faith with them would be through sacramental signs.[16] The connection of image, symbol and ritual speaks directly to the modern methods of visual, auditory and kinaesthetic learning which fill school classrooms.

There is research which suggests that, in the light of the accelerating culture,[17] modern generations of young people have less interest in spirituality. The temptation is that those outside of those 'target' generations only pay attention to the peripheral signs of that generation: at the Xboxes or the tattoos or the early sexualization, without delving too deeply into the culture and values which shape

14 The modern term for what we might better know as 'Assembly'.

15 J. W. Berryman (1999), *Godly Play: An Imaginative Approach to Religious Education*. Minneapolis: Augsburg Fortress.

16 C. Erricker (2007), 'Children's Spirituality and Postmodern Faith', *International Journal of Children's Spirituality*, 12(1), 51–60.

17 J. Gardner (2008), *Mend the Gap: Can the Church Reconnect the Generations*. Nottingham: IVP.

these external manifestations.[18] The process of quizzing young people in itself may generate a false image as many are willing to take up contrary positions just to be 'young'. In the classic 1953 film *The Wild One*, an authority figure asks a really cool Marlon Brando, 'What are you rebelling against, Johnny?', to which he replies, 'Whaddya got?'

The ambivalence towards religion is, I would suggest, more about apathy towards the established shape of Christianity than a rejection of the gospel itself and lends itself to the opportunity to proclaim afresh in *each and every generation* the Good News of Jesus Christ, which must be prepared and contextualized to each new generational challenge.

That there are such distractions as social networking, interactive video-gaming and ever more bizarre forms of self-gratification should not be a matter of fear, but a new series of tools for those tasked in mission to reach out through these new media.[19] When Vincent Donovan worked with the Masai[20] he described a missional context which applies powerfully to our work with children and young people: that effective mission springs from listening to them and then helping them to discover for themselves a life of faith.

This might mean that their sacramental life eventually looks a little different from that of previous generations: connected and yet in an evolved shape. I would suggest that the sacraments of previous generations, cultures and communities were similarly a little different from where we are today; and that this is an evolving response to the continuing revelation of God.

It will not be up to us, as the previous generations, to shape it, but to allow it form and function and to enable the DNA of the sacramental life to be passed on and given new meaning and context. There will still be sacraments, and the intrusion of the divine in our mundane will always ensure that God will be revealed in new and exciting ways to young people!

---

18 S. Savage, S. Collins-Mayo, B. Mayo and G. Cray (2006) *Making Sense of Generation Y: The World View of 15–25 year olds*. London: Church House Publishing.

19 D. Adams (1999), 'How to Stop Worrying and Learn to Love the Internet', http://www.douglasadams.com/dna/19990901-00-a.htmlm, accessed 22 March 2011.

I suppose earlier generations had to sit through all this huffing and puffing with the invention of television, the phone, cinema, radio, the car, the bicycle, printing, the wheel and so on, but you would think we would learn the way these things work, which is this:

1) everything that's already in the world when you're born is just normal;

2) anything that gets invented between then and before you turn thirty is incredibly exciting and creative and with any luck you can make a career out of it;

3) anything that gets invented after you're thirty is against the natural order of things and the beginning of the end of civilisation as we know it until it's been around for about ten years when it gradually turns out to be alright really.

Apply this list to movies, rock music, word processors and mobile phones to work out how old you are.

20 V. Donovan (1982), *Christianity Rediscovered*. London: SCM Press.

3

The Power of Storytelling

We love stories. Stories are at the heart of community. They link people and they pass on values, ideas and a sense of connection from one generation to the next.

The Christian faith is, at its heart, a collection of stories that seek to bring us closer to the heart of God. It is a heart which we forget at our peril, for in the drive to apply twenty-first century rigour to ancient stories, in the desire to *know* authentically whether something is simply true or not, then we lose the true sense of what Holy Scripture is trying to tell us.

Karen Armstrong reminds us of the relationship between fact and myth:

> In most pre-modern cultures there were two recognised ways of thinking, speaking and acquiring knowledge. The Greeks called them *mythos* and *logos*. Both were essential and neither was considered superior to the other ... each had its own sphere of competence and it was considered unwise to mix the two.[21]

Logos equates with 'reason' and enabled people to function effectively in the world. It had therefore to correlate with the tangible reality around us. *Logos* was therefore essential to our human survival.

> ... but it had its limitations: it could not assuage human grief or find ultimate meaning in life's struggles. For that, people turned to *mythos* or 'myth' ... Today we live in a society of scientific *logos* and myth has fallen into disrepute. In popular parlance, a myth is something which is not true. But in the past, myth was not a self-indulgent fantasy; but rather like *logos*, it helped people to live creatively in our confusing world ... a primitive form of psychology.[22]

21 K. Armstrong (2009), *The Case for God*. London: Bodley Head, p. 3.
22 Armstrong, *The Case for God*, p. 3.

It is wrong therefore to assume that something which firmly belongs to the mythical genre is not true, but is truer in a real sense, for it seeks to make sense of the world. Nowhere is this seen more vividly than in the Holy Scriptures.

The sacramental life is not separate from Scripture, rather it feeds and grows from Holy Scripture. The criticism of many outside the catholic perspective is that the sacramental clouds the message of Scripture, whereas I want to assert that Scripture is a tool of illumination for the revelation of God in sacramental form.

It is therefore essential that any book on the sacramental life reflects on the sacramental purpose of Scripture and the stories that underpin the revelation of Christ in yet another mystical form. Pete Ward in his book *Mass Culture* speaks of the Eucharist as a storytelling event, an exploration of the missional story at the heart of the gospel.[23]

And yet, in many churches, and in much work with young people, the Bible has been reduced to either a second-rate form of entertainment or something with the inspirational capacity of a *Haynes Manual*.[24] Scripture is a living, breathing entity with the power to capture imaginations, and this is primarily because for most children these stories are almost entirely unknown.

In both my Collective Worship and in small group work, it is very clear that most young people now lack the basic framework of the Christian story. Their points of reference are more likely to be a Disney movie or a cartoon than a Bible story. The cultural baggage of Christmas (i.e. Santa, reindeer and the movie *Elf*) or Easter (eggs and bunnies) cloud the real message of these essential Christian festivals: it was once overheard between two mothers in the playground 'Two weeks off for Easter – I don't know, it's a lot of fuss for a chocolate egg …'

This lack of insight places the storyteller at a certain disadvantage, for the reliance on *retelling* was much easier for the storyteller than in telling the story for the first time. However, with a little imagination we can see that this is the real mission opportunity: to place the hearer into the encounter for the first time, and to inspire and retell the teachings of Christ and his marvellous (in the sense of making us marvel at them) deeds, as though we were there ourselves.

The Synoptic Gospels were originally oral accounts, only latterly committed to paper, and they contain the vibrancy and intimacy of being there.[25] Read them

---

23 P. Ward (1999), (ed.), *Mass Culture*. Oxford: Bible Reading Fellowship.

24 For those outside the UK, a *Haynes Manual* is an extremely useful collection of technical drawings and step-by-step instructions for motor vehicles. They are excellent for what they do, but the plots are a little thin and the characterization leaves much to be desired.

25 Why else would the Evangelist remark that the five thousand sat down on the green grass (Mark 6.39) if he was not there?

in a disinterested, dispassionate voice and you lose the real sense of what they were intended to convey: a transformative encounter with Jesus.

My technique for storytelling therefore is heavily based around a first-person account: for example as a disciple: Peter, James or John – a witness to the events, often retold in modern language and transferring the story to a modern setting. The Good Samaritan can so easily be transferred to a story of football tribalism, for example.[26]

Movie Clips – the Box of Tricks

Stories can be retold in a variety of ways, and there is a huge bank of clips which can be used to illustrate biblical stories. Films and TV series such as *The Miracle Maker*[27] or the *Story Keepers*[28] can be easily edited to tell a specific story.

If you do use video clips from either Christian or secular films, then you should seek the appropriate licence for their use. Christian Copyright Licensing International (CCLI) provide a video licence which should cover most eventualities and can sit alongside the CCLI music licence. Further information on the CCLI Video Licence can be found at http://www.ccli.co.uk/licences/churches_showing-films.cfm. However, the perfect clip might not always be available, or the nuance of the story not to your needs, and so you find yourself with the need to retell the story yourself. A good way of creating such stories in child-accessible ways is using animation.

Animation – Telling the Story

Of course, people of all ages love animation: the magical telling of a story through moving drawings or acted out with figurines. Children are especially drawn to them, and it is perhaps for this reason that animation is overwhelmingly seen as a childish pursuit. I think this is fundamentally wrong, but through telling a story in animation, eternal truths can be shared among all generations.

Not everyone can draw confidently enough or have the multi-million-pound computing hardware or the Disney Pixar Studios to create animation, but in this section I want to share some techniques which are not difficult but which can be effectively used to tell the greatest stories of all time.

---

26 S. Rundell (2010), *Creative Ideas for Alternative Sacramental Worship*. Norwich: Canterbury Press, pp. 124–6.

27 http://www.imdb.com/title/tt0208298/, accessed 19 March 2011.

28 http://storykeepers.com/, accessed 19 March 2011.

Stop-frame Animation

Stop-frame animation is usually animation with models, although it can also be used to build a movie out of hand drawings. Not all stop-frame animation has to be as complex as *The Miracle Maker*.[29] One can easily create simple but effective animations with Barbie Dolls, Action Men, Lego characters,[30] those little life-dummies which can be obtained from art shops, or even Plasticine. All you need is a digital camera and a basic tripod, a table and a couple of reading lamps to provide an even light.

A Typical Stop-frame Setup

This example uses a low-end digital SLR with a standard lens, but a standard digital camera has also produced very effective results. The tripod, even a small table-top tripod, is essential and keeps the whole thing stable.

As with normal photography or video, the secret to making an interesting shot is in filling the frame. Go close! Zoom in on a facet of the model or a close head shot rather than sticking with wide angle shots which lose detail. There is a place for wide angle to set the scene, but for the most part, the closer the better.

---

29 *The Miracle Maker* is an exquisite, child-friendly story of Christ told in animation and is ideal for showing either complete or in excerpt form to teach key elements of the ministry of Jesus.

30 See http://www.youtube.com/watch?v=rZVjKlBCvhg, Eddie Izzard's brilliant 'Church of England – Cake or Death?' routine. Teenagers love this. Accessed 9 February 2011.

A close-up generates more engagement with the story.

For the animation of a drawing, place the tripod directly over the drawing, in as even a light as you can create.

Take off the automatic flash: it's too bright, especially for these kinds of close-ups, and use the light generated by your table lamp. Reading lamps can be directed. Try to minimize shadows. You will be surprised as to how close you are to the image.

You will be surprised at how close you are to the image.

To animate, take either one or two pictures ('frames') in a single position, then move the model slightly. Take another one or two frames. Move it. Repeat.

More convincing action can be when more than one figure or limb moves at the same time – an arm and a head, two figures together or an expression and a limb. Experiment to see how much of your model needs to move each frame

The movement available is often limited by the flexibility of the model. Some dolls can only raise and lower their arms and turn their heads. This is fine, as recording this kind of movement can be used effectively to tell the story. As the characters turn their heads: shake or nod, raise an arm to point to something. Once the reading is recorded over this animation, you will find that it makes sense.

For a conversation between two characters, I often film a couple of different shots in one go, rather than setting up each shot individually. This greatly helps with the continuity of a shot. You can edit them together at a later stage.

Some animators have had particular success with superimposing moving mouths over the inert faces of their characters[31] but this is quite difficult. It is possible to record a close-up of a real mouth talking and to use a 'mask' to isolate this mouth close-up before superimposing it. It's not that hard to do, but looks very impressive.

If you look at the animation examples folder of the CD, you will see examples of different shots and the attempts to make the shots look like those you would film, This makes them more realistic. To understand more about masking, why not search for a tutorial on the Internet, such as the excellent *Little Rich* tutorials for Sony Vegas on YouTube.

You will discover the benefits of additional tape or Blu-tack as you build your animation, especially when out of sight, to ensure that models are not knocked over, or hold items correctly or stay in just the right position.

Once you have your collection of single frames, you need to make them into a single movie. I use a marvellous free utility which can be downloaded from http://www.jarrin.net/JPG_to_AVI.html.

---

31 http://www.youtube.com/watch?v=VhdGR_nPtow, accessed 9 February 2011.

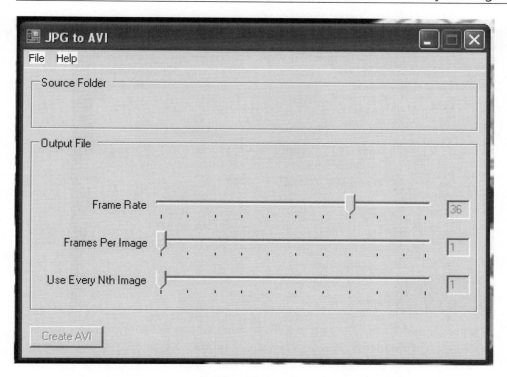

This small program converts a series of photographs into a movie. You can then further manipulate that in the standard video-editing tools which come with your computer (for example, Windows Movie Maker or iMovie) by adding sound or commentary.

If you place your characters in front of some bright green card or paper, then you have the opportunity to add a different background (known, not surprisingly, as 'green screen' or more technically as 'chromakey') in some more sophisticated video packages (such as Sony Vegas).

Using JPG_to_AVI to Animate a Toy

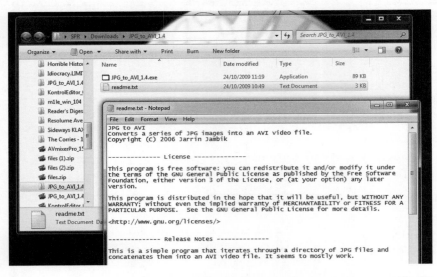

The program does not have an install, so you can just run it straight from where you have downloaded it. It works best on Windows XP.

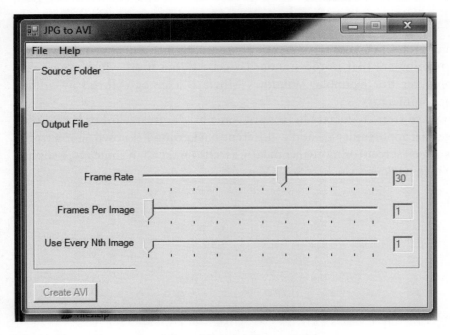

This is the main screen. Select *File* and *Open Folder*

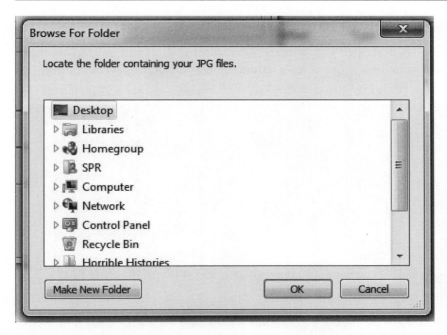

and browse to the folder where your sequentially numbered camera shots are stored.

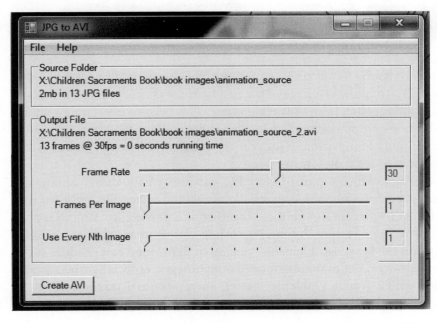

Click on the 'Create AVI' button and your animated sequence will be created.

Drawn Animation

The techniques described above as stop-frame animation can be transferred to drawn animation by the use of a rostrum tripod and smooth, even lighting.

I have found that by fixing an A4 pad to the table using strong tape and working backwards, using the last page of the pad first, I was able to make a series of drawings, faintly tracing from the previous one. This became effectively a photographed flip-book animation and created a beautiful effect. Children are used to creating this kind of animation in the corners of their school exercise books and so are delighted to see it on screen.

Windows Paint, which is part of every PC, can create basic drawn animation: one just saves each frame as a sequentially numbered image file and then uses the JPG_to_AVI program to knit them together as a movie clip. A more sophisticated drawing tool such as Adobe Photoshop can dramatically improve this technique, and the low-cost 'Elements' version of Photoshop can produce excellent original drawings or manipulations of other images, especially when used in conjunction with a graphics tablet for better, finer, more artistic control.

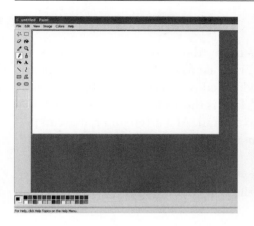

1. Windows Paint is on every PC.

2. Draw a simple stick man and at the end of each drawing, *Save As* a different sequentially numbered file, i.e. *file1.jpg, file2.jpg.*

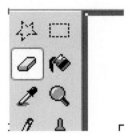

3. Use the *Eraser tool* to remove elements of the drawing.

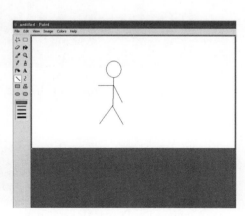

4. Like this ...

5. Redraw and Save As a new image.

The Digital Rostrum Camera

When one has a number of static images – classical pictures of biblical scenes, for example,[32] or a drawing – these can still be used for an engaging and dramatic story using a common feature of most video editing packages: what is usually called something like 'crop and zoom'.[33] This is the ability to add an image to a video-editing package and pull in close to a detail. At a given point, one can pull out to reveal more of the picture, or pan across the image to another character or detail.

I find that this technique works best when one records the soundtrack first, and then fits the images to the telling of the story.

An Illustration of the Rostrum Camera in Sony Vegas

1. Import the images from your hard disk into the media window.

---

32 A great resource site for these images is Artcyclopedia, http://www.artcyclopedia. com/, accessed 19 March 2011, which is an index site for the world's prestigious art collections and can retrieve the best art of the past 1,000 years in high quality.

33 Windows Live MovieMaker can be downloaded for free from http://explore.live.com/ windows-live-movie-maker, accessed 19 March 2011.

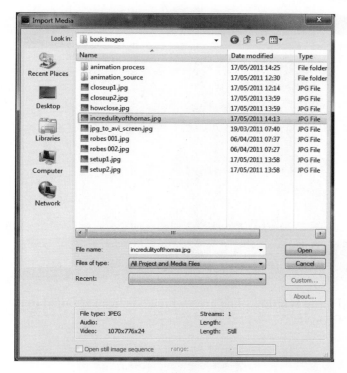

2. Select your images.

3. Drag the image down onto the timeline and select the Pan and Crop option which is at the middle right-hand side (the top icon) of the picture itself.

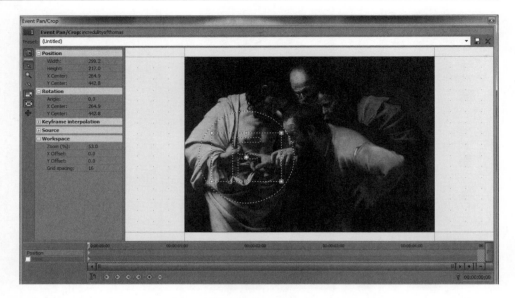

4. This opens the Pan and Crop window. The area which has been zoomed in is marked by the box with 'F' on it.

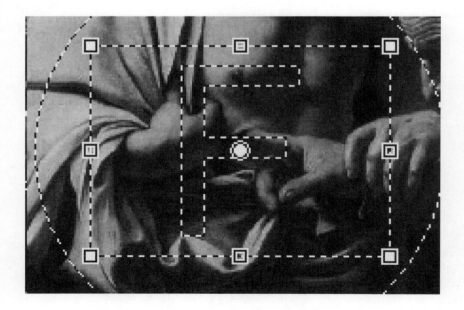

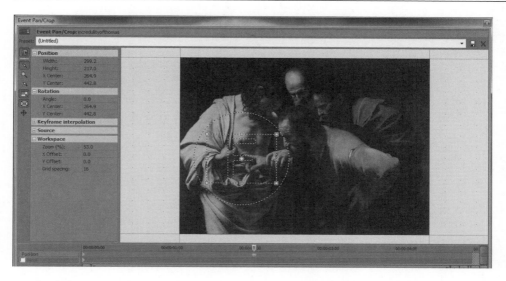

At the bottom on this window is the timeline. At present, this marks the beginning point of the view.

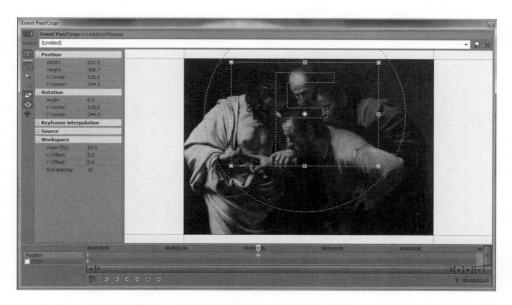

By clicking to a point on the timeline, and resizing the 'F' box, the view on screen will smoothly move between these two points, panning and zooming as required. This means that a loving movement down an image, or a reveal from a detail to a wider shot or a zoom in to make a point, may be choreographed very easily.

By laying down the audio first, it is very easy to lay out the necessary zooms and pans over a static graphic which invites the viewer into an engagement with what would otherwise be a very static image.

4

Liturgies

My major principle is that the source of all creativity is the Holy Spirit working through you, and that your liturgy should be a reflection of both who you and your gathered community are and your charism. However, one does recognize that sometimes good, creative ideas need an external spark, so I have drawn together in this chapter some ideas to stimulate you. This includes complete liturgies and many fragments for you to draw upon for a variety of settings: Sunday worship, special children's services in church, youth clubs, school Collective Worship ('assemblies') and intimate informal youth worship in the context of discipleship.

Adopt, adapt and improve: it's all God's and it's all in the service of the gospel.

EUCHARIST

Liturgy is a dynamic, not a static, entity. It is a communication between God and people, and because people change and reform before the unchanging God, the liturgy itself must be reinvented constantly to reflect their journey and their growth, based upon the past and looking to the future. This is one of the reasons why I regard the tying down of liturgy to a single prayer book, a single form of 'acceptable' words, to be inappropriate. When a commission or a committee seek to police the liturgy, then creativity is stifled. I have long been arguing for an Order 3 in *Common Worship* which is entirely rubric based and leaves the words and rituals to the worshipping community while firmly placing it in a framework which is drawn from the breadth of the Christian tradition. The Canons of the Church of England do recognize that variation and creativity are good, and Canon B5 allows some flexibility within the guidance of the bishop.

The graffiti artist Banksy[34] once said that it is easier to seek forgiveness than

---

34 http://www.banksy.co.uk.

it is to seek permission. If our liturgies are creative, innovative and yet still correspond to the shape of the liturgy, and are done in sincerity and authenticity, then the liturgical police should not come knocking at your door in the middle of the night.

Making Eucharistic Vestments

As part of teaching about the Eucharist, we begin with the naming and identification of the various eucharistic vestments worn in church. On a set of stickers are the names of the vestments (chasuble, alb, stole, amice, etc.). There is a wonderful opportunity to strip the priest and label his garments before the whole congregation! This is followed up with the designing of a chasuble and stole for a favourite teddy or doll. It gives the young people the opportunity to consider some of the signs and symbols used in church and in relation to the Eucharist, including bread, wine, lambs, grapes, crosses and other seasonal symbols.

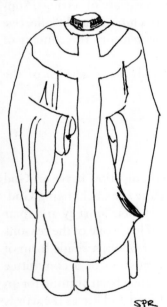

SPR

For the purposes of this exercise, it was found that a Gothic-style chasuble was the most useful design.

Our designs were made in paper and created for the toys. We were then able to play with liturgical processions as the children bore their teddies and dolls. One design was chosen and the young people then created their symbols in a larger form on fabric using fabric pens or fabric paints (available from any craft or art shop) and these were then appliqued (stitched) onto a larger chasuble and stole fabric.[35]

The result was a set of eucharistic vestments which were owned by the children: designed and made by them, and which are now used at many acts of worship and not necessarily for those exclusively for children.

---

35 Templates for the adult-sized vestments can be found in B. D. Baumgarten (2002) *Vestments for All Seasons*. London: Continuum International Publishing Group, p. 128.

Lesson Plan: Vestments

Question: Why does our priest wear such funny clothes?
Answer: Because these clothes signify that they are doing God's work. When they wear these clothes, everyone can see that they are to do something very special – leading the people of God (you and me) in prayer and the sacraments.

Plan: Today we are going to learn about what our priest wears and what they are called so that we can make some for them to wear.
Activity 1: Diagram.
Activity 2: Teddy demo.
Activity 3: Make for small teddies.
Activity 4: Recap practice with signs.

Liturgical Colours

Purple: penitential, preparation, Lent, Advent.
Black: sad, Good Friday, funerals, requiems.
Red: blood, martyrs, Pentecost (flames).
White: happy, Easter, Christmas, sacraments.
Green: Ordinary Time, God's creation.
Pink: Mothering Sunday, Refreshment Sunday in Advent.

Questions and Answers Before the Eucharistic Prayer

New Patterns for Worship[36] discussed using the kind of dialogue used in the Jewish Seder or Passover meal, where the youngest member in the family asks questions which give meaning and context to the action which is to follow. This is further explored later in this chapter in a full Seder Meal liturgy. We evolved this idea to meet our community's distinctly sacramental perspective and to give emphasis to the doctrine of the Real Presence in the Eucharist.

Q. Why do we give thanks and praise to God?
A. Because he has created all that is, and he has given us life. He is the reason behind everything, and yet loves each and every one of us.

Q. Why do we remember Jesus?
A. Because Jesus was sent from God, stepping into this world as one of us, while remaining God. Jesus gave up his life for us on the cross and was raised from the dead so that we might see that death is not the end, but the beginning of a new life: the life Jesus showed us how to live.

Q. Why do we use bread?
A. Because Jesus took bread at the Last Supper, and said it became him. Jesus becomes present here and he feeds us as we share in him with others around his holy altar. From one bread we all become united as his children.

Q. Why do we use wine?
A. Because as Jesus said at the Last Supper: this wine becomes his blood: a sign of Jesus' saving love, poured out for us when he died on the cross.

A simpler alternative might be:

Q. Who are we remembering and who is here with us?
A. Jesus Christ the Lord who lives today.

Q. Why do we take this bread?
A. To show that his body was given up to death for us.

---

36 *New Patterns for Worship* (2008), London: Church House Publishing.

Q. **Why do we take this wine?**
A. To show that Jesus shed his blood for our sins.

Q. **Why is there one loaf and one cup?**
A. Because we are one family; we belong to each other like the parts of a body.

Q. **Why do we come to his table?**
A. He invites us because he accepts us. We are his people and we share in his heavenly life.

Q. **For how long will Christians celebrate like this?**
A. Until Jesus comes to take us to be with God in heaven.

Adapted from *New Patterns for Worship*.[37]

Eucharistic Prayers

I have always preferred to seek out the best prayers and worship to use in the right context, which has often taken me outside of the boundaries of liturgy strictly (and legally) enforced within my own church. If the best prayer can be found in the prayer books of another Anglican church (which carries therefore a *commended* status with the Church of England and is therefore not quite as illegal) or in the Roman Missal or in a Reformed Church, then I believe that it can and should be used, and it can be further adapted for the needs of those with whom you are worshipping and to reflect the charism and theology of your own church. There are Canons in Church of England Law which allow for local and pastoral use.[38]

However, there are times when nothing else quite hits the mark, and it is then that you should not be afraid to create something authentic for your own community. I recall a priest who held a Communion service in a school each week and wrote a special preface each week which reflected the life and experience of the school, the news and the lives of the children. This narrative brought the celebration firmly within their experience and offered their lives, hopes and dreams to God in worship.

All Eucharistic Prayers follow a common framework. In their fullest form they are in this shape:

37 *New Patterns for Worship*, p. 42.
38 Canon B5, Canons of the Church of England, http://www.churchofengland.org/media/35588/complete.pdf, p. 20, accessed 20 May 2011.

- **Opening Praises** – a call and response framing the worship.

- Preface – a themed narrative which itself has a distinct shape:
  - Words of praise and worship.
  - **The core theme of the preface.**
  - Drawing in the worship of the whole community of faith.

- **Sanctus and Benedictus** – invoking the words of worship of the angels and the saints adapted from Isaiah 6.3.

- **Invocation of the Holy Spirit and *Epiclesis*** – sending the work of the Spirit through the priest into the eucharistic elements (although in Orthodox-influenced prayers, this occurs after the Institution Narrative).

- **Institution Narrative** – recalling the words and actions of Jesus at the Last Supper.

- Memorial Acclamation – a responsory which recalls the salvific work of Christ and the promise of the resurrection.

- Anaphora – Thanksgiving Prayers.
  - That we are able to gather together in worship.
  - For the mighty saving works of Christ.

- Intercessory Prayers.
  - Praying for the Community of Faith, its leaders.
  - Gathering the intercessions of the angels, saints (especially the Saint of the Day), prophets and patriarchs alongside those of Mary, the mother of Jesus.

- **Doxology** – worship and adoration.

- **Great Amen** – the assent of the community of faith.

Items in bold cannot really be dispensed with.

With this structure in mind, it is possible to weave a wonderful series of narratives which explore the Eucharist. The following examples of prefaces have been written for use in school with children aged between seven and eleven years of age. You can modify the language to suit each age group. These prefaces work especially well with the Anglican Eucharistic Prayers later in this section.

At the Start of a School Year

The Lord be with you.
And also with you.

Lift up your hearts.
We lift them to the Lord.

Let us give thanks to the Lord our God.
It is right to give thanks and praise.

Father, almighty and ever-living God, we begin our school year by coming to you in thanks and praise.

As we look forward to a year of hope, of challenge, of new opportunities and new beginnings, we know that you are with us to guide and support us, saved by the sacrifice for us of your Son, Jesus Christ our Lord, and sustained by the power of the Holy Spirit.

We thank you for bringing us together as a school community and look forward to all that this year will bring.

So we join our prayers with all the angels, saints, prophets, patriarchs and the whole company of heaven as we sing to your glory.

Holy, Holy, Holy ...

At the End of the School Year

The Lord be with you.
And also with you.

Lift up your hearts.
We lift them to the Lord.

Let us give thanks to the Lord our God.
It is right to give thanks and praise.

Father, all-powerful and ever-living God, we delight in coming together to worship you in the power of the Holy Spirit through your beloved Son, Jesus Christ our Lord.

We give you thanks and praise for all we have shared over this school year. We have walked in faith with you, felt your love and received your many blessings in our lives.

We have laughed and played, cried and been comforted, explored your wonderful world and heard of your outstanding love.

So we join our prayers with all the angels, saints, prophets, patriarchs and the whole company of heaven as we sing to your glory.

Holy, Holy, Holy …

In Response to a Tragedy or Sadness in the School

The Lord be with you.
And also with you.

Lift up your hearts.
We lift them to the Lord

Let us give thanks to the Lord our God.
It is right to give thanks and praise.

Father, all-powerful and ever-living God, hear us we offer our prayers to you, through your Son, Jesus Christ our Lord.

As we try to make sense of what has happened within our school community, we are reminded that as Jesus hung upon the cross he won for us an everlasting victory over sin, death and everything which makes us sad.

The resurrection shows that Jesus can make all things new, and although we share in the sadness of this time, we look towards a new beginning and a restoration in hope.

You promise us that in times of great sadness you will wipe away all of our tears, and so we join our prayers with all the angels, saints, prophets, patriarchs and the whole company of heaven as we sing to your glory.

Holy, Holy, Holy …

South African Eucharistic Prayer

This Eucharistic Prayer, which is inspired by a prayer created for the Anglican Church of the Province of Southern Africa, takes the questions of an individual child or group of children and spreads them through the whole prayer. This piece of liturgy could spark a whole series of commentary and questions through the sacramental acts, especially with baptism. The underlined questions may be asked by one or a series of different children.

The Lord be with you.
And also with you.

Lift up your hearts.
We lift them to the Lord.

Let us give thanks to the Lord our God.
It is right to give thanks and praise.

Q. Why do we give thanks and praise at this table?

We give thanks for all that God has done for us.

God the Father created the heavens, the earth and everything in them; and created us in his own image.
Let us give thanks and praise.

Christ our Lord became human like us, and died to save us.
Let us give thanks and praise.

God sent the Holy Spirit to gather us together as the people of God.
Let us give thanks and praise.

So come, let us join together to worship this God who loves us.

Holy, holy, holy Lord, God of power and might, heaven and earth are full of your glory, hosanna in the highest. Blessed is he who comes in the name of the Lord. Hosanna in the highest, hosanna in the highest.

We praise you, Father, that before Jesus our Saviour died, he gave us this holy meal.

Q. Why do we eat bread together at this table?

On the night before he died, Jesus took bread. After giving thanks he broke it, and gave it to his disciples saying, 'Take, eat. This is my body, given for you. Do this in remembrance of me.'

Q. Why do we drink from the cup together at this table?

In the same way, after supper Jesus took the cup, saying, 'This cup is God's new covenant sealed with my blood, poured out for you for the forgiveness of sins. Do this in remembrance of me.'

Q. What do we remember at this table?

We remember the Father's gracious love for us, Christ's death and resurrection for us, and the Spirit's tender care for us.

Let us proclaim the mystery of faith.

Christ has died,
Christ is risen,
Christ will come again.

Merciful Father, pour out your Holy Spirit on us and on these gifts of bread and wine. In eating and drinking together may we be made one with Christ and with one another.
Amen.

Anglican Style Eucharistic Prayers

A series of Eucharistic Prayers especially for children were presented before the Church of England General Synod after much work from the Liturgical Commission, the committee which formulates Church of England liturgy. They were distributed around the dioceses and used in churches experimentally. Unfortunately Synod rejected them. This is a great pity because I think they were particularly good, vivid and work with children. They are seasonal, picking up on the theme of the time of year. We should remember that Parliament rejected the 1928 Prayer Book which was also rather good.

The following two prayers have been developed along lines which were inspired by those prayers.

Prayer 1

This prayer features a number of seasonal variations.

The Lord be with you.
And also with you.

Lift up your hearts.
We lift them to the Lord.

Let us give thanks to the Lord our God.
It is right to give thanks and praise.

It is always right to give you thanks and praise
God our Father,
holy and strong,
holy and immortal,[39]
King for ever.

Through your Son
you made us
and the whole universe.

Advent, Christmas and Epiphany
Your Holy Spirit came to Mary,
and Jesus was born as one of us.

Lent
When his time had come,
Jesus suffered and died on the cross
to save us from our sins.

Easter
When his time had come,
Jesus suffered and died on the cross.
On the third day
you raised him from the dead
and crowned him Lord of all.

---

39 A reference to the Trisagion, an ancient Orthodox-influenced prayer.

School Beginning
We look forward to the beginning of this school year
filled with hope and expectation,
seeking to do our best
and share in your love.

School End
We give you thanks for all we have shared this year,
our achievements, our joys,
our challenges and sadness,
knowing that each step you have walked with us
as we grow and learn and share.

Ordinary Time
Your Holy Spirit came to Mary
and Jesus was born as one of us.
When his time had come
he suffered and died on the cross
to save us from our sins.
He broke the chains of death
and returned to you in glory.

You send your Spirit
to bring new life to the world
and fill us with power from on high.

And so we join on earth
with all the angels, saints, prophets and patriarchs in heaven
to praise your name and sing:

Holy, holy, holy Lord,
God of power and might,
heaven and earth are full of your glory,
Hosanna in the highest.
Blessèd is he who comes
in the name of the Lord.
Hosanna in the highest.

Father, as we remember
the death and resurrection of your only Son,
⁺send your Holy Spirit
that the bread and wine we bring before you
may be for us Christ's body and his blood.

So Father, on the night before he died
Jesus had a special meal with his friends.

He took bread and thanked you,
he broke it and gave it to them saying:

'Take this all of you and eat it, this is my body
given for you. Do this to remember me.'

[*Bells*][40]

After the meal, Jesus took the cup of wine.
He thanked you, gave it to them and said:

'Drink this all of you. This is my blood,
the new covenant of God's love.
Do this to remember me.'

[*Bells*]

Jesus Christ has died,
Jesus Christ has died.
Jesus Christ is risen,
Jesus Christ is risen.
Jesus Christ will come again,
Jesus Christ will come again.

---

40 Bells! In *our* tradition! Why not? The original purpose of bells in church was to draw attention to the important things that were happening: the start of the service, the Eucharistic Prayer and the presentation of the elements to the people. 'Pay attention!' is the message. I notice that children (and adults) do indeed pay attention to what's happening when a bell is rung. Can you imagine a coherent theological reason why bells should *not* be rung at these high points in the liturgy?

Pour your Spirit on us
that we may live as children of your heavenly kingdom.
Help us to love one another
as we work for peace, justice
and wait for Jesus to come again in glory.

For all honour and glory belongs to you, heavenly Father,
through Jesus Christ your Son
with the Holy Spirit:
one God now and for ever.
Amen.

Prayer 2

This prayer returns to the question-and-response style featured elsewhere.

The Lord be with you.
And also with you.

Lift up your hearts.
We lift them to the Lord.

Let us give thanks to the Lord our God.
It is right to give thanks and praise.

Why is it right to give thanks and praise?
Because God is love and does wonderful things.

Lord of all life,
you created the universe
where all living things reflect your glory.
You give us this great and beautiful earth
to discover and to take care of.

One of the following may be used.

You give us the stars and the sky above,
the sun and the moon,
and everything that gives us light
to enlighten our eyes and hearts and minds.

or

You give us fish in the sea,
the birds in the air,
and every plant and tree:
the life that sleeps in the earth in winter
and awakens again in the spring.

or

You give us parks and schools
and places to play,
shrieks of laughter
and safety in your arms.

[*In times of sadness*]
You give us your love
even when things go wrong.
Jesus knew hurt and pain.
Through him you wipe away our tears
and fill us with your peace.

[*In times of celebration*]
You give us happy times
and things to celebrate.
In these we taste your kingdom,
a feast for all to share.

You made us all
each wonderfully different,
unique and special
to join with the angels and saints,
and the whole company of heaven
to sing your praise:

**Holy, holy, holy Lord,
God of power and might,
heaven and earth are full of your glory,
Hosanna in the highest.
Blessèd is he who comes
in the name of the Lord.
Hosanna in the highest.**

We thank you loving Father
because you sent Jesus your Son.
He gave his life for us on the cross
and shows us the way to live.

We ask you now to +send your Holy Spirit
that these gifts of bread and wine
may be for us Christ's body and his blood.

Why do we share this bread and wine?
Because Jesus makes them signs of his love.

On the night before he died,
when darkness had fallen,
Jesus took bread.
He gave thanks, broke it
and shared it with his disciples.

'This is my body,' he said,
'given for you.
Do this to remember me.'

After they had eaten, he took the cup,
gave thanks and shared wine with his disciples.

'This is my blood,' he said,
'poured out for you and for all
to save them from their sins.
Do this to remember me.'

Father, with this bread and this cup
we celebrate his love, his death, his risen life.
As you feed us with these gifts,
send your Holy Spirit upon us all
and change us more and more
to be like Jesus our Saviour, brother and friend.

Why do we follow Jesus Christ?
Because he is God's saving love in action.

Help us to love one another
and to work together for that day
when the whole world is fed,
suffering is ended
and all creation is gathered into your loving arms.

With all your saints
we give you glory
through Jesus Christ
in the strength of the Spirit
for ever and ever.
Amen.

Roman Eucharistic Prayers for Children

Shortly after the Church of England Synod rejected a series of special Eucharistic Prayers for Children, a member of the Liturgical Commission was asking me how it might affect my work with children in eucharistic worship. I told her frankly that it wouldn't have that much effect because until the Church of England approved proper ones, I would fall back on the following two.

Prayer 1

The Lord be with you.
And also with you.

Lift up your hearts.
We lift them to the Lord.

Let us give thanks to the Lord our God.
It is right to give thanks and praise.

God our Father, you have brought us here together so that we can give you thanks and praise for all the wonderful things you have done.

We thank you for all that is beautiful in the world and for the happiness you have given us. We praise you for daylight and for your word which lights up our minds. We praise you for the earth, and all the people who live on it, and for our life which comes from you.
We know that you are good. You love us and do great things for us.

So we all sing (say) together:

Holy, holy, holy Lord,
God of power and might,
heaven and earth are full of your glory.
Hosanna in the highest.

Father, you are always thinking about your people; you never forget us. You sent your Son Jesus, who gave his life for us and who came to save us. He cured sick people; he cared for those who were poor and wept with those who were sad. He forgave sinners and taught us to forgive each other. He loved everyone and showed us how to be kind. He took children in his arms and blessed them.

So we are glad to sing (say):

Blessed is he who comes
in the name of the Lord.
Hosanna in the highest.

God our Father, all over the world your people praise you. So now we pray with the whole Church: with *N* our bishop. In heaven the blessed Virgin Mary, the apostles and all the saints always sing your praise. Now we join with them and with the angels to adore you as we sing (say):

Holy, holy, holy Lord,
God of power and might,
heaven and earth are full of your glory.
Hosanna in the highest.
Blessed is he who comes
in the name of the Lord.
Hosanna in the highest.

God our Father, you are most holy and we want to show you that we are grateful.
We bring you bread and wine and ask you to send your Holy Spirit to make these gifts the body ⁺and blood of Jesus your Son.

Then we can offer to you what you have given to us.

On the night before he died, Jesus was having supper with his apostles. He took bread from the table. He gave you thanks and praise. Then he broke the bread, gave it to his friends and said:

'Take this, all of you, and eat it:
this is my body which will be given up for you.'

When supper was ended, Jesus took the cup that was filled with wine. He thanked you, gave it to his friends and said:

'Take this, all of you, and drink from it:
this is the cup of my blood,
the blood of the new and everlasting covenant.
It will be shed for you and for all
so that sins may be forgiven.'
Then he said to them: 'Do this in memory of me.'

We do now what Jesus told us to do. We remember his death and resurrection and we offer you, Father, the bread that gives us life and the cup that saves us. Jesus brings us to you; welcome us as you welcome him.

Let us proclaim the mystery of faith:

**Christ has died,
Christ is risen,
Christ will come again.**

Father, because you love us, you invite us to come to your table. Fill us with the joy of the Holy Spirit as we receive the body and blood of your Son.

Lord, you never forget any of your children. We ask you to take care of those we love, especially of N and N, and we pray for those who have died.

Remember everyone who is suffering from pain or sorrow. Remember Christians everywhere and all other people in the world.

We are filled with wonder and praise when we see what you do for us through Jesus your Son, and so we sing:

Through him, with him, and in him, in the unity of the Holy Spirit, all glory and honour are yours, almighty Father, for ever and ever.
Amen.

Prayer 2

The Lord be with you.
And also with you.

Lift up your hearts.
We lift them to the Lord.

Let us give thanks to the Lord, our God.
It is right to give thanks and praise.

Thank you, God our Father.
You made us to live for you and for each other.
We can see and speak to one another,
and become friends,
and share our joys and sorrows.

And so, Father, we gladly thank you with every one who believes in you; with the saints and the angels, we rejoice and praise you, saying:

Holy, holy, holy Lord,
God of power and might,
heaven and earth are full of your glory.
Hosanna in the highest.

Blessed is he who comes
in the name of the Lord.
Hosanna in the highest.

Yes, Lord, you are holy;
you are kind to us and to all people, for this we thank you.

We thank you above all for your Son, Jesus Christ.
You sent him into this world
because people had turned away from you
and no longer loved each other.

He opened our eyes and our hearts
to understand that we are brothers and sisters
and that you are Father of us all.
He now brings us together to one table and asks us to do what he did.

Father, we ask you to bless these gifts of bread and wine and make them holy.
Change them for us into the body ⁺and blood of Jesus Christ, your Son.

On the night before he died for us,
he had supper for the last time with his disciples.
He took bread and gave you thanks.
He broke the bread and gave it to his friends, saying:

'Take this, all of you, and eat it:
this is my body which will be given up for you.'

In the same way he took a cup of wine.
He gave you thanks and handed the cup to his disciples, saying:

'Take this, all of you, and drink from it:
this is the cup of my blood,
the blood of the new and everlasting covenant.
It will be shed for you and for all people
so that sins may be forgiven.'

Then he said to them:

'Do this in memory of me.'

God our Father,
we remember with joy that Jesus died to save us.
In this holy sacrifice,
which he gave as a gift to his Church,
we remember his death and resurrection.

Father in heaven,
accept us together with your beloved Son.
He willingly died for us,
but you raised him to life again.
We thank you and say:
Glory to God in the highest!

Jesus now lives with you in glory, but he is also here on earth, among us. We
thank you and say:
Glory to God in the highest!

One day he will come in glory,
and in his kingdom
there will be no more suffering,
no more tears, no more sadness.
We thank you and say:
Glory to God in the highest!

Father in heaven, you have called us to receive the body and blood of Christ at this Table and to be filled with the joy of the Holy Spirit. Through this sacred meal give us strength to please you more and more.

Lord, our God, remember N our bishop before you.
Help all who follow Jesus to work for peace and to bring happiness to others. Bring us all at last together with Mary, the Mother of God, and all the saints, to live with you and to be one with Christ in heaven.

Through him, with him, in him, in the unity of the Holy Spirit, all glory and honour are yours, almighty Father, for ever and ever.
Amen.

Nursery Rhyme Mass

Brian Ogden wrote a wonderful collection of nativity plays for infant school-age children[41] which featured fun songs set to the tunes of well-known nursery rhymes. For younger children this is firmly within their culture, and for older children it can be seen as ironic fun. This Eucharist takes that idea and places it firmly within the sacramental liturgy, but would not have been possible without Brian's original genius idea.

Gathering

(*To the tune of 'Here We Go Round the Mulberry Bush'*.)

We gather round in this holy space,
holy space, filled with grace.
We gather round in this holy space
to do what Jesus taught us.

---

41 B. Ogden (2002), *Nursery Rhyme Nativities*. Oxford: Barnabas/BRF.

We hear the stories of Jesus, our King.
Eternal life, for us he'll win.
We share his meal and pray with him
and do what Jesus taught us.

In the name of the ⁺Father, and of the Son and of the Holy Spirit.
Amen.

Penitential Rite

(*To the tune of 'Ba Ba Black Sheep' or 'Twinkle, Twinkle'.*)

Just like lost sheep we have gone astray,
done bad things and run away.
So we come to say sorry,
make things better as you see.
Loving Jesus make anew
our lives so we can be like you.

Absolution

(*To the tune of 'If You're Happy and You Know It'.*)

You're forgiven and you know it, so clap your hands,
you're forgiven and you know it, so clap your hands,
you're forgiven and you know it, so you really ought to show it,
you're forgiven and you know it, so clap your hands.

Jesus loves you and you know it, so stamp your feet,
Jesus loves you and you know it, so stamp your feet,
Jesus loves you and you know it, so you really ought to show it
Jesus loves you and you know it, so stamp your feet.

If you believe that God forgives you, say 'We do' 'We do',
If you believe that God forgives you, say 'We do' 'We do',
When you say that you are sorry, you no longer have to worry,
God takes away your sin, so say 'Amen'. **Amen!**

Collect

(Of the day/season/Sunday/festival.)

Word

(Of the day/season/Sunday/festival.)

Prayers

(To the tune of 'London Bridge is Falling Down'.)

We thank you Lord for all we have,
all we have, all we have.
We thank you Lord for all we have,
which you give us.

We pray to you for all our friends,
all our friends, all our friends.
And all those who need our prayer,
come and help them.

We pray for those who are sick or ill,
sick or ill, sick or ill,
Sad or lonely, stressed or ill,
come and help them.

Hail Mary, full of grace,
full of grace, full of grace.
The Lord is with you, pray for us
Now and always.

And to you we give our prayers,
give our prayers, give our prayers.
Hear us Lord and help us on,
now and always.
Amen!

Peace

(To the tune of 'This Old Man'.)

Here we are,
one in Christ,
gathered here,
Ain't this nice?
So let us share a sign of peace,
a kiss or hug before the feast ...

The peace of the Lord be always with you.
And also with you.

We share a sign of peace.

Eucharistic Prayer

(To the tune of 'Kumbaya'.)

The Lord is here right now.
His spirit is with us.

Lift up your hearts to him.
We lift them up.

It's the right thing to do.
Yes, Jesus.
Oh yes, we come in prayer.

It is right, O Lord
that we come
to worship you
in thanks and praise.
We gather here,
hearts and minds,
knowing that
you're here with us.

Holy, holy Lord, O holy God,
our prayers are joined
by the saints.
Blessed is the one
who comes in peace.
Blessed is the Prince of Peace.

⁺Send your Spirit, Lord
on these gifts
so they may be to us
Christ's flesh and blood.
As we share in them
may he be with us
and save us by these heavenly gifts.

On that night
that he was betrayed
he took the bread
and gave God thanks.
'Take this and eat
of my flesh',
it will become that bread of life.

[*Bells*]

And then he took
the cup of wine.
He gave God thanks
and bid us drink.
'This is my blood
I spill for you.
It is a sign that all is new.'

[*Bells*]

Let us proclaim
of our faith.
'Christ has died
and has arisen.
Christ will come
to us again.
O yes, he will return.'

And we join
our prayers here now,
angels and saints
and all in heaven
with Our Lady
and all on earth.
So we pray as one voice:

Amen, Amen.
Let it be so,
Amen, Amen.
Let it be so,
Amen, Amen.
We say this now,
Amen, O yes, Amen!

Lord's Prayer

(*To the tune of 'Jack and Jill'.*)

Our Father, who art in heaven,
hallowed be thy na-a-ame.
Thy kingdom come,
thy will be done,
on earth as it is in heaven.

Give us today our daily bread,
forgive us all our si-i-ns,
as we forgive
all those us who sin
or trespass against us.

Let us not be drawn into
any kind of temptation.
Deliver us
from the evil one.
Amen, Amen, Amen.

Agnus Dei

(*To the tune of 'Three Blind Mice'.*)

Lamb of God, Lamb of God,
you take away the sin of the world.
Have mercy on us, Lamb of God.
Don't let us stray away from the flock.
You take away the sin of the world,
so grant us peace.

Come and eat, come and drink,
you're welcome here, come quite near.
Share in his body and blood with us,
it tastes like wine and bread but just
know that inside it's not like that.
Share the food of God.

[*Communion and blessings are distributed.*]

Post Communion Prayer

(*Of the day/season/Sunday/festival.*)

Blessing and Dismissal

(*To the tune of 'Sing a Song of Sixpence'.*)

May the Lord now +bless you
and keep you all safe,
send you out from here
in a state of grace.
Take what we have learned
about Jesus our King,
and do what he has taught us
to make the world a better thing.

Go, the Mass has ended
but our service has begun.
We heard it straight from Jesus
what it means to live as one.
With him now up in heaven
looking from above,
blessing us in all our work,
let's go and share his love.

Amen.

Eucharist in Rhyme

Simple words for complex ideas. I can sense the spirit of Dr Seuss in this text, the difference being that this isn't nonsense.

The Lord is here.
In this place.

It makes us feel great inside.
To be with him.

Let's do this now.
As Jesus told us to.

Send your Spirit
⁺on these gifts,
bread and wine
so they shine
with your love.

Take and eat,
taste and see
the Lord is good,
the Lord is good.

Take this bread
from the field,
take this bread.
He said 'for this is me'.

Take this wine
from the vine,
it's a sign
his blood in wine.

Christ has died,
Christ is risen,
Christ will come again.

Thanks and praise,
thanks and praise
to you we raise.

Joining our prayer
with all you there
in heaven
with us on earth.

All the saints
and your mum,
all the living
and the gone.

We share your love,
we share your food,
we share you
with all our friends.

So thanks and praise
to you we raise.
Amen, Amen, Amen.

Tweet Eucharist #twucharist

The concept of Twitter is well understood by many young people: 140 character messages which form part of a never-ending flow of information, reflections, matters of interest and thoughts for reflection. The purpose of this is not to take the intimate gathering of community which is at the heart of the Eucharist and spread it into a disconnected multiverse, but rather to simplify the often wordy and indeed over-wordy words of the Eucharist and to make them easily identifiable and significant.

In this celebration with young people, we simultaneously project the words of each message on the screen, while sending them out via the social networking site, Twitter (where they are known as 'Tweets'). The key to this is the simplification of language, which draws us closer to the action present.

The use of the # or hashtag enables the following of a given topic, in this case the celebration itself; it also signifies key stages in the eucharistic shape.

In Dr Seuss's *Green Eggs and Ham*,[42] Theodore Guisel writes an entire book using just 50 words, 49 of which are of only one syllable.[43] I am not sure it is possible to translate a Eucharist into one-syllable words, but that spirit is in this text.

I did try to summarize the whole thing into one tweet, but that hardly justified people coming out for it in the evening. That was:

#twucharist #sorry #forgiven #jesus #word #here #take bread & wine #send spirit #remember jesus #break #pour #share #thanks #amen

So here is the full version:

#twucharist #gather Father, Son, Spirit.
#twucharist Here.
#twucharist Welcome. God is here. Make yourselves at home.
#twucharist #confession – We first pause to turn from wrong.
#twucharist Lord have mercy.
#twucharist Christ have mercy.
#twucharist Lord have mercy.
#twucharist #absolution You are forgiven. You are loved.
#twucharist #collect Let us pray ... Heavenly Father, your Son was the living word, made flesh & here among us ...
#twucharist #collect ... May we set aside our busy lives, noise & fuss to focus on the true word.
#twucharist #collect ... Your Son, Jesus Christ our Lord, who with the Holy Spirit is all the one true, great God of all.
#twucharist #collect Amen.

42 Dr Seuss (1960), *Green Eggs and Ham*. London: HarperCollins.

43 The word list is: a am and anywhere are be boat box car could dark do eat eggs fox goat good green ham here house I if in let like may me mouse not on or rain Sam say see so thank that the them there they train tree try will with would you. The only multi-syllabic word is, of course, 'anywhere'.

#twucharist #word Listen: John 1.1–2.

#twucharist The Word was first, the Word present to God, God present to the Word. The Word was God, in readiness for God from day one.

#twucharist Everything was created through him; nothing – not one thing! – came into being without him.

#twucharist What came into existence was Life, and the Life was Light to live by. The Life-Light blazed out of the darkness;

#twucharist ... the darkness couldn't put it out.

#twucharist For the gospel of the Lord – Thanks be to God.

#twucharist God is here. Make yourselves at home.

#twucharist Lift up your hearts ... we lift them to God.

#twucharist Give thanks ... For it's the right thing to do.

#twucharist #thanksgiving In ways we do not understand, in ways we cannot hope to understand, Christ is present in our midst,

#twucharist ... a living word: dying & rising & continuing to live forever. Here.

#twucharist All the millions of words of theologians, prayers of saints or witness of the apostles have not got their heads around this.

#twucharist We can't see the wind, but we know what happens to the trees. Look not for the wind, but the effect of the wind.

#twucharist We can't see any outward change in bread & wine, but we know by these prayers something is different.

#twucharist Look not for God hiding under an ordinary piece of bread as St Francis said but look for the effect on those who share it.

#twucharist Bread: simple, wholesome, good – the staple of life & proof in our hands of God's bountiful goodness to us all.

#twucharist Wine: source of joy & gladness, an example of God's love in a glistening drop of rich, dark sweetness.

#twucharist Our prayers echo the song of the angels, saints, prophets & patriarchs & the whole company of heaven as we say ...

#twucharist #sanctus Holy, Holy, Holy Lord, God of power & might. Heaven & earth are full of your glory. Hosanna in the highest.

#twucharist Blessèd is he who comes in the name of the Lord.

#twucharist #holy You are holy. You are the fountain of all holiness.

#twucharist Send your spirit on these gifts so bread & wine can become the actual body & blood of Christ.

#twucharist On the night he died, he gathered like us with his friends.

#twucharist With this bread: 'Take & eat. This is my body. Given for you.'

#twucharist With this wine: 'Come & drink. This is my blood. An agreement in blood. A deal for your sin. Do this to bring me present here.'

#twucharist #mystery It is a mystery: Christ has died. Christ is risen. Christ will come again.

#twucharist It's good.

#twucharist It's changed.

#twucharist And through it we are changed.

#twucharist You won't find Jesus wedged between the crumbs, but he is there.

#twucharist He gives himself to us in this way, so we can get our heads around the enormous idea of God stepping into this world.

#twucharist He gives himself to us, so that we may become a part of him.

#twucharist You eat food. It becomes a part of you.

#twucharist You eat of this & you become a part of him. A Holy Communion, at one with God.

#twucharist The only thing we can do is respond in love & joy, awe & wonder.

#twucharist May all of us who taste this foretaste of heaven be brought together as your Church on this earth.

#twucharist May we remember all those not with us & bring us all into your holy presence, through the powerful & mighty saving work of Jesus.

#twucharist Through him, with him, in him, in the unity of the Holy Spirit, all glory & honour are yours, almighty Father, for ever & ever.

#twucharist Amen.

#twucharist dad @ hvn, ur special,we want wot u want,Earth 2b like hvn,Giv us food & 4giv us,Lik we 4giv uvaz,don't test us,Save us!bcos we kno ur the boss,ur tuf & ur cool, 4eva.ok[44]

#twucharist #come Come. Share. Eat at God's table.

#twucharist No one is turned away. No one is unworthy. All are welcome.

#twucharist #share Be thankful. Be changed. Be aware that God is in our midst.

#twucharist #share.

#twucharist #after By this meal, we have been changed.

#twucharist Through bread & wine transformed into the body & blood of Christ you have been healed, restored, renewed.

#twucharist You have been fed for life's journey with something more than a snack. You have been fed with the stuff of life.

#twucharist The food of this earth just makes you hungry again.The food of this meal will last forever.This bread & wine are for all time.

#twucharist #blessing You have been fed for life's journey, you are blessed by God. Go from this place filled with God's spirit.

#twucharist #amen.

---

44 This one is more than 140 characters, I admit. In practice I would split it in two, but the unity of the prayer should not be undermined for this text.

Memorial Acclamation in Action

Christ has died (arms out on the cross).

Christ is risen.

Christ will come again! Hurrah!

The best part of this is that you can teach it and forget all about it while it remains in the memories of the children. Weeks after this was used, in the middle of a full parish Mass, the standard (said) memorial acclamation was used, and from the pews in which the Sunday School sat there came a resounding 'Hurrah!' – an outbreak of joy which should be at the heart of this memorial acclamation for us all. It takes children in our midst to sometimes remind us all of the joy and vitality of the Christian faith.

The Lord's Prayer

Although the words of the Lord's Prayer are probably the closest to our hearts, we must always need to perceive them as being in translation, and as such we need to recognize that so many translations in some way fall short of the beauty or glory of Christ's teaching as recorded in Matthew 6.9–13 or Luke 11.2–4. The use of relevant translations therefore for children, which speak to them and their idiom, is, I believe, both justified and necessary for teaching: so that they might understand what they are praying. In *Eastenders* a character called Tiffany lets slip that she always thought God's name was 'Harold' because of the Lord's Prayer: 'Our Father, who art in Heaven, Harold be thy name ...'[45]

45 http://blogs.mirror.co.uk/we-love-telly/2010/10/quotes-of-the-week-96.html, accessed 6 February 2011.

However, I am of the firm belief that once they understand the significance and meaning of the Lord's Prayer, they should be encouraged to learn and internalize a traditional form, so that they might join the wider praying community, and it can allow grandparents and grandchildren from 4 to 110 to pray together alongside all ages in between.

Text Language

The challenge is to get it into 160 characters.

> dad@hvn, ur special,we want wot u want,Erth 2b like hvn,Giv us food & 4giv us,Lik we 4giv uvaz,don't test us,Save us!bcos we no ur the boss,ur tuf & ur cool,4eva.Ok

A Translation By Children

Reinterpreted by Jack, India and Harry from the Parish of St Thomas the Apostle, Elson. How would your young people express the prayer in ways that they might understand?

> Our dear God, who lives in heaven,
> your name is very, very special and great.
> You look after everyone who has died and everyone alive.
> We want to live here on earth, with you, just like you live in heaven.
> Please give us all that we need to survive.
> Sorry for all we've done wrong – please forgive us.
> We will forgive everyone who has done wrong to us.
> Please stop us wanting to do bad things and don't let anything bad hurt us or make us want to fight back.
> Help us to remember that you made this planet, and us, and everything else on it.
> You are in charge of the world and will be for ever.
> Amen.

Benediction of the Blessed Sacrament

We shouldn't worry about whether children 'understand' the gentle worship and meditation which is at the heart of the Benediction of the Blessed Sacrament, because, put simply, who does? The capacity of young people for quiet and reflection in the presence of the Blessed Sacrament cannot be underestimated.

Benediction traditionally uses a number of quite inaccessible hymns, and yet there exists a whole genre of charismatic choruses which are filled with the same sense of adoration and worship which is at the heart of eucharistic devotion. Some might consider the use of such charismatic material in this deeply sacramental way quite ironic. One wonders what the writers, given their quite different theological position, might think if they knew how we use it. I hope that they would be enlightened and recognize that, at the heart of it all, is the worship of Almghty God which is the same across all the church traditions. One of my favourites is the song 'My Jesus, My Saviour' by Darlene Zschech, which when read slowly and meditatively in the presence of the Blessed Sacrament is perfect praise of Jesus in his sacramental form.

In the following liturgy there are a number of song suggestions. Select one from each section, or choose your own suitable tracks. They can be played live, or used from a CD. Permission for use of the songs can be obtained through the CCLI licence.

Equipment for Benediction

- A Monstrance – an often highly ornate method for displaying the Blessed Sacrament which has been previously consecrated and stored in your church's tabernacle or aumbry. Although they are often made of gold and highly expensive, they can be obtained from overseas craftsmen in more cost-effective materials for a fraction of the price via eBay.
- Consecrated Host – Jesus is most definitely needed for this devotion!
- Thurible and Incense – if you do not have a thurible, then a balti dish with sand in it makes a very cost-effective static place to burn incense. Charcoal sticks to burn in the thurible can be obtained from any church supplies shop, and I suggest the use of a long-handled spoon[46] to keep the charcoal free from ash. A chef's blow-torch is another excellent tool in the thurifer's kit as it enables charcoals to be lit quickly and evenly. When people complain about

---

46 The very best implement for scraping and preparing the thurible is a pair of hospital forceps: the Spencer-Wells which look like a pair of scissors and enable you to safely pick up or scrape the charcoal.

the choking nature of incense burning, it is usually not the incense which causes a problem but the spent ash from charcoal. The trick is to remove that ash and to blow on the charcoal to make it red/white hot before receiving a fresh hit of incense. This makes the burning sweeter and avoids the carbon monoxide which makes people cough.

- Humeral Veil – an often ornate piece of cloth worn around the shoulders of the priest to emphasize a separation of priest and sacrament, which is really the purpose of all eucharistic vestments. Children might like to design one as part of their eucharistic vestments.

In this liturgy, there is a three-person team referred to as 'sacred ministers'. Benediction is usually given by a priest, but young people make excellent other sacred ministers: a thurifer and a Master of Ceremonies who is on hand to assist the priest, place on the humeral veil and ring the bells during Benediction itself.

Gathering

Suggested music:

'Our God is Here' by Chris Muglia.[47]
'How Great is our God' by Chris Thomlin.[48]
'Glorious' by Chris Thomlin.[49]

The Blessed Sacrament is placed in the monstrance and then placed upon the altar which is festooned with candles. If you do not have traditional candlesticks for Benediction, then I suggest just using a large number (10 or 16) tea lights.

---

47 'Our God is Here' by Chris Muglia, downloadable from http://www.spiritandsong.com/products/30100388, copyright © 2001 Sound Mission Music. Published by spiritandsong.com.

48 'How Great is our God' by Chris Thomlin, downloadable from http://www.musicnotes.com/sheetmusic/mtdVPE.asp?ppn=MN0051994, copyright © 2004 worshiptogether.com songs/sixsteps Music, admin. by EMI Christian Music Publishing.

49 'Glorious' by Chris Thomlin, downloadable from http://www.musicnotes.com/sheetmusic/mtd.asp?ppn=MN0055943, copyright © 2005 worshiptogether.com songs, admin. by EMI Christian Music Publishing/sixsteps Music (admin. by EMI Christian Music Publishing).

Exposition and Adoration

Suggested music:

'My Jesus, My Saviour' by Darlene Zschech.[50]
'King of Kings, Majesty' by Jonathan Veira.[51]

Incense is added to the thurible. The sacred ministers kneel and the incense is offered to the sacrament.

Meditation

We gather here in this sacred space, in this quiet and reflective space which is separate from the busyness and the bustle of our lives. We have come to meet with Jesus, who wants to be come and be with you. In our hearts. In our lives.

On our altar is the reason for our gathering: Jesus.

Don't be distracted by the many flickering candles or the ornate and fancy gold object which is before you. Yet, look closely at it, it's what we call a 'monstrance' and you will see displayed at the centre an ordinary piece of bread, which through the prayers of a priest has become the body of Christ.

Whenever we gather together as the people of God in the Mass, the prayers of the priest and the responses of the people bring Christ into our midst. In ways in which we do not understand, or could ever hope to understand, Christ is present in our midst. The many thousands, millions of words of theologians, the prayers of saints, the witness of the apostles: *none* of them have ever got their heads around what happens here.

We can't see the wind, but we know what happens to the trees. Look not for the wind, but for the effect of the wind. We can't see any outward change in the bread of the altar, but we know that something is different. Look not for God hiding under an ordinary piece of bread, as St Francis once said, but look for the effect on those who share in the body and blood of Christ and come as we do now, to pray with him.

---

50 'My Jesus, My Saviour' ('Shout to the Lord') by Darlene Zschech, downloadable from http://www.musicnotes.com/sheetmusic/mtd.asp?ppn=MN0049440), copyright 1993 Hillsong Publishing.

51 'King of Kings, Majesty' by Jarrod Cooper, downloadable from http://www.jesusreigns.co.uk/sheetfiles/KingOfKingsMajesty.zip, copyright Sovereign Lifestyle Music.

In our quiet prayers we can bring to him all that makes us sad, all that makes us anxious, all that is on our minds. We can bring him our joys and celebrations, our hopes and our fears. For Jesus, with us here, is ready to listen. To you. To want to be with you, to share your story, and help you.

Lord Jesus, we open our hearts to you and pray that we may be able to recognize you in our lives. Bless us and walk with us, all the days of our lives.

Amen.

Worship

Suggested music:

'Be Still for the Presence of the Lord' by David Evans.[52]
'Facedown' by Matt Redman.[53]

At the first verse of 'Be Still' or the first chorus of 'Facedown', the sacred ministers prostrate themselves. They then rise and incense is added to the thurible; the sacred ministers kneel. The sacrament is censed again.

Collect

Let us pray.

Almighty God, you left us in this sacrament a reminder of your love poured out for us. Help us, we pray, as we worship you through the mysteries of your body and blood. May we come to know what you won for us on the cross. We know you are alive in heaven, our King, our God. Amen.

The humeral veil is placed on the priest so that they give the blessing of Benediction without touching it, and so we can focus on Jesus and not on the priest.

Benediction

The priest gives a blessing with the monstrance, and the people respond to that blessing with the sign of the cross as bells are rung and incense is offered.

---

52 'Be Still for the Presence of the Lord' by David Evans, downloadable from http://www.musicnotes.com/sheetmusic/mtdVPE.asp?ppn=MN0059292), copyright © 1986 Kingsway's Thankyou Music.

53 'Facedown' by Matt Redman, downloadable from http://www.musicnotes.com/sheetmusic/mtdVPE.asp?ppn=MN0054101, copyright 2003 Survivor (Kingsway's Thankyou Music).

Reposition

The Blessed Sacrament is taken from the monstrance and placed back in the tabernacle or aumbry.

Suggested music:

'Strength Will Rise' by Chris Thomlin.[54]
'Let Everything that has Breath' by Matt Redman.[55]

BAPTISM

Children and Baptism

The traditional age of infant baptism – below one year of age – is becoming increasingly rare as parents bring toddlers and older children (often in a 'package deal' with other children) or as a part of preparation for a wedding. We must ask ourselves how to respond positively and pastorally. These children, more than mere babes in arms, are no longer passive recipients of the sacrament of baptism. We should therefore strive to include children presented for baptism in ways that are meaningful for them, that promote their inclusion while not diminishing pastorally the commitment and promises that parents and Godparents are expected to make on their behalf.

For adults, we have no problem with asking them the question, 'Do you wish to be baptized?' and 'Is this your faith?'[56]

So, it should be common courtesy to ask this of a six-year-old. It should of course, not be asked out of the blue. At that age, one would have expected them to have been in some way involved in their baptism preparation, and had an idea of what was about to happen so that they understood that this was the reason the whole family were gathering, as the implications of a child refusing baptism do not bear thinking about.[57]

---

54 'Strength Will Rise' as performed by Chris Thomlin, downloadable from http://www.musicnotes.com/sheetmusic/mtdVPE.asp?ppn=MN0067615, Brenton Brown and Ken Riley, copyright 2005 Kingsway's Thankyou Music.

55 'Let Everything that Has Breath' by Matt Redman, downloadable from http://www.musicnotes.com/sheetmusic/mtdVPE.asp?ppn=MN0067615), copyright © 1997 Kingsway's Thankyou Music.

56 *Common Worship: Baptism.* London: Church House Publishing, pp. 66, 71.

57 Although it might be worth considering what usually happens when a child old enough to give an informed response is not asked, and the baptism is performed amid a complete kerfuffle of tears, kicking and screaming. Is this any better or any less abusive?

The Baptism of Siblings

From holding books (because as I explain, the priest doesn't have three hands) to candles, there is much at a basic level that can involve young people gathered at the baptism of a sibling. I often seek to go beyond that and involve even quite young siblings in the sacramental tasks of anointing their brother or sister with both the oil of baptism and the oil of chrism. Even young children are able to tell the difference between the two oils.[58]

This anointing can get playful and messy, which is good, simply because good religion is messy and abundant in grace, symbolized by copious amounts of oil smeared around.

Telling the Story – A Liturgy for Baptism

There is so much to say about baptism that there are not enough books in the world to carry them. No amount of baptism preparation, I find, ever fully captures all that needs to be said about the mystery of baptism. Baptismal teaching should also therefore be at the heart of each celebration of the Sacrament so that all those attending (both children and adults) may have an insight.

This running commentary can be tailored for any age group that you want to target, knowing that all the adults will respond to a children's explanation far more readily than if you presented it to them directly.

Welcome

In the name of the ⁺Father and of the Son, and of the Holy Spirit.
Amen.

The Lord be with you.
And also with you.

We gather together today for a very special reason: to celebrate the baptism of N. It's a day of joy when we come together as family and friends in order to see the marvellous things that God has done in his/her life and also in our own lives.

---

58 Hint: it's in the smell – the oil of baptism is unfragranced whereas the oil of chrism is the oil of royal and priestly anointing and is highly perfumed.

After words of welcome, the priest begins the service with the Collect for Baptism.

Let us pray.

Heavenly Father,
by the power of your Holy Spirit
you give to your faithful people new life in the water of baptism.
Guide and strengthen us by the same Spirit,
that we who are born again may serve you in faith and love,
and grow into the full stature of your Son, Jesus Christ,
who is alive and reigns with you in the unity of the Holy Spirit
now and for ever.
Amen.

Baptism is such a wonderful gift that we actually don't have enough words to express it properly, and when the words run out, as they always do, we turn to other ways of showing that: we might have been able to draw a picture, [and of course, we can sing a song as we already have], or we can do things, show things and share things in action which speak of these wonderful things: these symbols represent God's wonderful work in his sacrament of baptism and so we will use five symbols to try and in some way represent God's baptism.

But first, let's be clear about whom we are praying for in this baptism. I'm going to invite N, their parents and Godparents to come and stand with me here at the front of church.

Presentation

The priest asks those who are able to answer for themselves. I would person-ally ask this question of anyone over about the age of seven, even if parents and Godparents go on to answer on their behalf.

Do you wish to be baptized?
I do.

Or for infants, the child along with parents and Godparents are presented to the congregation:

Now, as we all know, it's a difficult job to be a parent or a Godparent. It's a job that they can't simply do on their own: they need the love, the support and the prayer of you – their family and friends; and so before I ask them these really important, demanding questions, I have a very important question to ask of you all …

To the whole congregation:

Faith is the gift of God to his people. In baptism the Lord is adding to our number those whom he is calling. People of God, (*that's you*), will you welcome this child/these children and uphold them in their new life in Christ?
With the help of God, we will.

To the parents and Godparents:

Parents and Godparents, the Church receives this child/these children with joy. Today we are trusting God for their growth in faith. Will you pray for them, draw them by your example into the community of faith and walk with them in the way of Christ?
With the help of God, we will.

In baptism this child/these children begin their journey in faith. You speak for them today. Will you care for them and help them to take their place within the life and worship of Christ's Church?
With the help of God, we will.

Decision

Baptism is an important decision, made by ourselves or on behalf of the children in our care.

> Parents and Godparents, the questions I am going to ask of you now are probably the most important questions I will ever ask anyone. Because *N* is unable to answer for *him/her*self, I ask you on their behalf, and with you rests the responsibility to live out these life-changing promises.

In baptism, God calls us out of darkness into his marvellous light. To follow Christ means dying to sin and rising to new life with him. Therefore I ask:

Do you reject the devil and all rebellion against God?
I reject them.

Do you renounce the deceit and corruption of evil?
I renounce them.

Do you repent of the sins that separate us from God and neighbour?
I repent of them.

Do you turn to Christ as Saviour?
I turn to Christ.

Do you submit to Christ as Lord?
I submit to Christ.

Do you come to Christ, the way, the truth and the life?
I come to Christ.

Oil of Baptism

The priest makes the sign of the cross on the forehead of each candidate with the oil of baptism. Parents and godparents also sign the candidates with the sign of the cross.

> The first of our symbols of baptism is the oil of baptism. It is a simple, unfragranced olive oil, made holy for us by our own bishop each Maundy Thursday, fresh each year. We use it to place the sign of the cross on the forehead of the person to be baptized. *(Allow young people to sniff the oil if they are willing.)* The cross is at the heart of our faith, a symbol of Christ and of what he did for us.
>
> The cross could so easily have been something to be ashamed of: a terrible form of torture, a very cruel treatment and a nasty way to die (point to the stained glass, crucifix or other visual representation of the crucifixion), and yet we are not ashamed of the cross, in fact we are very proud of the cross because it was not a sign of failure, but because of Christ's victory over sin and death through the cross it is a sign of triumph, a symbol that reminds us that nothing, not even death, can be stronger than the love of Jesus. So we wear that sign proudly …

Christ ⁺claims you for his own.
Receive the sign of the cross.

N, do not be ashamed to confess the faith of Christ crucified.
Fight valiantly as a disciple of Christ against sin, the world and the devil, and remain faithful to Christ to the end of your life.

May almighty God +deliver you from the powers of darkness, restore in you the image of his glory, and lead you in the light and obedience of Christ.
Amen.

> Our lives are a bit like a journey: throughout them we travel, and we grow. As we journey together, we might notice that we never travel alone, but that we travel with Christ at our side. To remind ourselves of this, we are going to make a short journey where we will encounter our second symbol. Come, parents and Godparents, let us journey to our font, as we continue our life's journey.

Water of Baptism

> Our next symbol is the sign of water. Water is essential for life. Without water we would quickly die.

Praise God who made heaven and earth.
Who keeps his promise for ever.

Let us give thanks to the Lord our God.
It is right to give thanks and praise.

We thank you, almighty God, for the gift of water
to sustain, refresh and cleanse all life.

Heavenly Father, +sanctify this water that, by the power of your Holy Spirit, all who are baptized in it may they be cleansed from sin and born again.

Renewed in your image, may they walk by the light of faith and continue for ever in the risen life of Jesus Christ our Lord;
to whom with you and the Holy Spirit be all honour and glory, now and for ever.
Amen.

> When we sign up for something really important like baptism, it is essential that we remember what it is that we are signing ourselves up for, to examine the small print, to make sure that we agree with the key principles of the Christian faith, so ...

Profession of Faith

Let us affirm, together with these who are being baptized, our common faith in Jesus Christ.

Do you believe and trust in God the Father, source of all being and life, the one for whom we exist?
I believe and trust in God the Father.

Do you believe and trust in God the Son, who took our human nature, died for us and rose again?
I believe and trust in God the Son.

Do you believe and trust in God the Holy Spirit, who gives life to the people of God and makes Christ known in the world?
I believe and trust in God the Holy Spirit.

This is the faith of the Church.
This is our faith.
We believe and trust in one God,
Father, Son and Holy Spirit.

The priest asks those who are able to answer for themselves:

Is this your faith?
This is my faith.

> When we talk of this, we often hear the word 'Christening' rather than the word, as it appears in the Bible – 'Baptism'. There is nothing wrong with 'Christening' for it is a fine old English word, but it sometimes carries with it the implication that it is here, at this service that N gets *his/her* 'Christian name'. However, N has been known by that name since *he/she* was born, and in fact the Holy Scriptures say that N was 'known before they were formed in the womb' (Jeremiah 1.5) and that God knows every hair on N's head (Luke 12.7), so the next part of our service recognizes not the naming of N, but their calling: calling by God, calling by name. God already knows us intimately by name and at this baptism he reaches out to N. He will call us at confirmation, on our wedding day, one to another, and even at the end of our lives; it is God who will call us by name back to be with him.

Therefore I ask, please name this child whom God is calling …

The parents are asked for the Christian names of the child.

Baptism

N, I baptize you in the name of the Father, and of the Son, and of the Holy Spirit.
Amen.

Our next symbol is the oil of chrism, which is again like the oil of baptism we used earlier – an oil made holy by our own bishop each Maundy Thursday. However, unlike the plain and simple oil of baptism, this oil is highly perfumed (encourage young people to sniff it). Three thousand years ago, when the people of Israel created kings, they didn't put a golden crown upon their heads, but rather doused them in this highly fragrant oil. They also used it to set apart their holy people; and in the same way, we use this oil to signal that baptism makes N very holy, very kingly/queenly, and gains membership of a royal family – the royal family of God in addition to their own loving family.

Oil of Chrism

The Priest smears the newly baptized with the oil of chrism as a sign of the outpouring of God's Holy Spirit.

The oil of chrism is a symbol of God's goodness to us and his grace, and recognizing that we don't use use a drop, but a whole load, poured out upon us like God's grace. Good religion is, of course, very messy.

We say together:

Through baptism, God anoints you with the chrism of salvation. As Christ was anointed Priest, Prophet, and King, so may you share everlasting life.

Robing in White

The newly baptized are draped in a white cloth to symbolize their new life with Christ.

Our next symbol is that of the white robe. In the fourth century those to be baptized would gather very early in the morning on Easter Day, just as the sun rose, just as Christ rose from the tomb (so see how kind I am to you!), gathering by the side of a river or the baptistry. There we (and it was usually adults who were baptized like this) would remove *all* of our clothes on one side of the river to symbolize putting away our past lives, and we would enter into the water as naked as the day we were born.

There in the water we would be baptized, and it was said that our old lives had died and we would be created as something new: a baptized person; and so we would rise up out of the waters of rebirth on the other side as someone 'born again' – it's not just the Americans who are 'born-again Christians' but everyone born of water and the Spirit (John 3.5). As the newly baptized rose out of the waters of baptism on the other side they would be clothed in a white robe to symbolize 'putting on Christ' and the purity which this baptism gave them.

To show this, we drape this white cloth around the shoulders of N to demonstrate their salvation won by these holy acts.

We say together:

You have been clothed with Christ.
As many as are baptized into Christ have put on Christ.

May God, who has received you by baptism into his Church,
pour upon you the riches of his grace,
that within the company of Christ's pilgrim people
you may daily be renewed by his anointing Spirit,
and come to the inheritance of the saints in glory.
Amen.

Welcome of the Faithful

There is one Lord, one faith, one baptism: by one Spirit we are all baptized into one body.

We welcome you into the fellowship of faith; we are children of the same heavenly Father; we welcome you.

Prayers

We pray for the newly baptized, their families, parents and Godparents.

> It is tough and challenging to be a parent, to be a Godparent, and so now we pray for N, and for you, that you may be supported in this wonderful, humbling, challenging task. Let us pray ...

Faithful and loving God,
bless those who care for these children,
and grant them your gifts of love, wisdom and faith.
Pour upon them your healing and reconciling love,
and protect their home from all evil.
Fill them with the light of your presence
and establish them in the joy of your kingdom,
through Jesus Christ our Lord.
Amen.

or

N, today God has touched you with his love
and given you a place among his people.
God promises to be with you
in joy and in sorrow,
to be your guide in life,
and to bring you safely to heaven.
In baptism God invites you on a lifelong journey.
Together with all God's people
you must explore the way of Jesus
and grow in friendship with God,
in love for his people,
and in serving others.

With us you will listen to the word of God
and receive the gifts of God.

In their name, in the Spirit of our common bond with Christ, let us pray together
in the words our Lord has given us:

Our Father, who art in heaven,
hallowed be thy name.
Thy kingdom come,
thy will be done,
on earth as it is in heaven.
Give us this day our daily bread.
And forgive us our trespasses,
as we forgive those who trespass against us.
And lead us not into temptation;
but deliver us from evil.

For thine is the kingdom,
the power and the glory,
for ever and ever. Amen.

Baptism Candle

Lit from the Paschal Candle.

Our final symbol is the symbol of the candle. Throughout this baptism this
large candle (it's known as the Paschal Candle) has been burning to remind
us of the presence of Christ here with us today.

To many, this world is a dark place, filled with all kinds of bad things and
the terrible things that people do to each other – in the playground, in wars
and all around the world.

Yet Jesus said that he was the light of the world (John 18.12), the light that
shines in the darkness (John 1.5). Even in the darkest of places, a single
light: the light from this Paschal Candle can shine out and make a difference. Each Easter Sunday we bring the new Paschal Candle into this dark
church to show how Jesus lights up our lives.

I believe that we have a little candle of faith within each and every one of us. If we were to light our candles of faith from the one true candle, Jesus, then we could turn off all the lights, and the dark and scary world would not be at all dark and scary, as our light, the light of Jesus would chase away the dark.

So, to remind N of this special day, I am going to take this baptism candle and light it from the candle of Jesus, the Paschal Candle. I recommend that you don't take this candle and put it in a drawer and forget about it: display it at home to remind the whole family of this special gift; and each birthday, I suggest you can do what we do, and put the baptism candle beside the birthday cake and light it, so as each year passes and the number of candles on the cake grows and grows, so the one candle, the candle of your baptism, N, remains constant, just as Jesus remains constant for you.

God has delivered us from the dominion of darkness and has given us a place with the saints in light. You have received the light of Christ; walk in this light all the days of your life.

Shine as a light in the world to the glory of God the Father.

Blessing

The God of all grace,
who called you to his eternal glory in Christ Jesus,
establish, strengthen and settle you in the faith;
and the blessing of God almighty,
the Father, the Son and the Holy Spirit,
be among you and remain with you always.
Amen.

Go in the peace of Christ.
Thanks be to God.

FUNERALS

Funerals are not in themselves sacramental, and so perhaps should not have a place in this book. However, because they do touch the lives of young people and it is increasingly recognized that young people can and should engage in celebrating the end of a loved one's life, this section will consider how they might want to take part in the funeral office.

Most emphatically, however, it is not about their performance, not about what they can do in a funeral service for the adults, but rather about how they might want to recognize the loss of a person close to them in a way that is meaningful for them.

An excellent work which is primarily orientated towards the funeral of a child is Sr Frances Dominica's *Just My Reflection*[59] which contains a wide selection of readings from Scripture, the Christian tradition and secular writings which have resonance with children.

I have often found that in funeral visits to a family, the direct and simple question asked by a child – 'Why did Granddad have to die?' – and the necessarily simple and direct response (which usually starts with an admission that I don't *really* know why) is the part of the visit that adults usually latch on to: simple truths explained simply go a long way.

Given the emotion of the funeral, it is often not pastorally right to expect a child to contribute a reading on the day, but I have often found that they want to stand alongside the priest or a relative as the older person reads what the child has written.

A better expression might be for a bereaved young person to respond in ritual: the placing of a photograph or picture they have drawn on the coffin, a reminiscence of a happy time shared with that loved one.

Remember Me

To the living, I am gone.
To the sorrowful, I will never return.
To the angry, I was cheated.
But to the happy, I am at peace.
And to the faithful, I have never left.
I cannot speak, but I can listen.
I cannot be seen, but I can be heard.

59 Sr Frances Dominica ASSP (1997), *Just My Reflection*. London: DLT.

So as you stand upon the shore,
gazing at the beautiful sea, remember me.
As you look in awe at a mighty forest
and its grand majesty, remember me.
Remember me in your hearts,
in your thoughts, and the memories of the
times we loved, the times we cried,
the battle we fought and the times we laughed.
For if you always think of me,
I will never have gone.

Anon.

WEDDINGS

In modern society, most priests encounter a situation which was unheard of a few years ago – where the couple to be married *even in their first marriage* have been life partners for many years already, live together and usually have children. It is no surprise therefore that a couple should want to involve their children, often as bridesmaids or pageboys.

Although this book is primarily about the liturgy of the sacraments, it is important to consider the pastoral role of the sacraments: the care and intimacy of a celebration of the Eucharist, the powerful pastoral effect of the ministry of healing which relies as much on the practice of priestly presence as on the administration of oil. In the same way, the Church should seek to use its sacramental life as a pastoral tool for the care and nurture of the people of God. This means walking with them and drawing them into a deeper relationship with God. It is not the place for judgement or condemnation, for Christ himself sought not to condemn.[60]

There is therefore a place and a purpose for recognizing the presence of children within a marriage. If children are part of that family already, I often insert the phrase 'continue to' into the Preface to the service to recognize that reality.

[Marriage] is given as the foundation of family life
in which children **continue to be** born and nurtured
and in which each member of the family, in good times and in bad,
may find strength, companionship and comfort,
and grow to maturity in love.

---

60 Matthew 7.1.

Traditionally, the roles of children in a marriage service have been restricted to the decorative: pageboys, bridesmaids and flower-girls. These are perfectly fine roles, and they are a delight to the wider family gathering. However, there is a place for them beyond that and the ritual of this sacrament beyond the handling of the ring cushion.

The Joining of Hands

N and M are joined together at this wedding not just one to another, but as a family. So I invite Cs, their children to come and join us at this point and as we join the newly ringed hands of N and M together and unite them all in the bonds of love and honour, surrounded by the blessing of the Church.

> In the presence of God, and before this congregation,
> N and M have given their consent
> and made their marriage vows to each other.
> They have declared their marriage by the joining of hands
> and by the giving and receiving of rings.
> I therefore proclaim that they are husband and wife.

> *As the right hands are joined together, the assembled children of the family also place their hands over the couples, and the priest wraps his stole around all of them, places his hand on the top and says:*

> Those whom God has joined together let no one put asunder.

Garlanded with Love

After the couple has been declared husband and wife, their children come forward with garlands of flowers and these are placed around the couple and the children.

> Jesus declared that he was the root of the vine, and we were the branches. You are joined together as a family with love. These stems surround you all: a mark of the love which enfolds you in each other, rooted in Christ. May you continue your growth and bear much fruit over the coming years.

CHRISTINGLE

The Christingle Service appears on church calendars any time from Advent Sunday through to the Presentation. Our particular tradition has been to hold it on Christmas Eve, and as it takes place around the time of the first Evensong of Christmas, it is effectively the beginning of Christmas proper.

Often the parish rallies around before the service to produce a number of Christingles to gently rot or be thrown away. One year, while struggling to make an enormous number, one bright spark[61] exasperatedly cried out, 'why don't we get the children to make their own next year?' It was indeed an idea of genius-level simplicity, and so now we still rally round to make not complete Christingles but a kit in a paper bag.

Christingle Kit

- Four cocktail sticks preloaded with raisins and dolly mixtures (you could get the children to create these themselves but as this involves sometimes quite young children, we always felt it was safer to pre-make these).
- A birthday candle and holder.
- An orange.
- A strip of red ribbon pre-cut to the right length.
- A copy of the Christmas Grace stapled to the outside of a paper bag to hold the kit.

The words of the Grace printed are:

Christmas Grace

(Light the Christingle and place it in the middle of the Christmas dinner table, or light a single white candle.)

Dear God,
May we whose faces shine from the light of your Christingle Candle
be blessed this Christmas, be blessed this year.
For family, for friends, for food and for all you do for us,
we give you praise!
Amen!

---

61 OK, it was Lorraine, my wife.

In this way we encourage the participants of the Christingle to replenish the sweets on the Christingle and to carry its purpose into the main family gathering and encourage a family to pray together on this most special day.

The readings are taken from a wonderful retelling of Bible stories called *Listen*[62] which is pitched perfectly for young children. It is now out of print, but I would recommend seeking it secondhand.[63]

Welcome

The priest enters the church from the back, counting down, which always seems to focus the congregation. It is even better when the children count down with you.

10 ... 9 ... 8 ... 7 ... 6 ... 5 ... 4 ... 3 ... 2 ... 1 ...

Christmas starts ... (*look at watch*) now! (*Cheers and whoops of joy.*)

Welcome to our Christingle Service!

In the name of the ⁺Father, and of the Son and of the Holy Spirit.
Amen.

The Lord be with you.
And also with you.

O Come All Ye Faithful

1   O come, all ye faithful,
      joyful and triumphant,
      O come ye, O come ye to Bethlehem;
      come and behold him,
      born the King of angels:

      O come, let us adore him,
      O come, let us adore him,
      O come, let us adore him, Christ the Lord!

---

62 A. J. McCallen (1980), *Listen: Themes from the Bible Retold*. London: Collins.
63 Your friend in finding secondhand, cheap or out-of-print books is Abe: http://www.abebooks.co.uk.

2   God of God,
Light of light,
Lo, he abhors not the Virgin's womb;
very God,
begotten, not created:
Chorus.

3   Sing, choirs of angels,
sing in exultation,
sing, all ye citizens of heaven above:
'Glory to God
in the highest:'
Chorus.

Now I won't keep you long tonight as I know you all have to get back to your beds because some of you may be expecting someone to call later.

However, before then, I want us tonight to go on a special journey.

There are so many of us that we can't actually move, but this will be a journey of the mind: a journey through the Christmas story, and through this journey I hope that we will be able to remind ourselves of the reason why we gather on this special night, the reason for the season, the story of the birth of Jesus Christ, our Lord and Saviour.

So, let us begin our journey by hearing what Isaiah foretold.

Listen to this:

A reading from the book of a wise man called Isaiah.

'Once upon a time, everyone lived in the dark,
but now – we can see!
They used to live in a world that was so full of shadows,
but now – we have a light to light up our way!

We have God with us
and he has made us happy.
He has sent us a baby
who is to be our King,
and he will keep everyone safe.

This is the word of the Lord.
Thanks be to God.

Let us now sing 'The First Noel' as we turn round to the sanctuary.

The First Noel

1   The first Nowell the angel did say
    was to certain poor shepherds in fields as they lay:
    in fields where they lay a-keeping their sheep
    on a cold winter's night that was so deep:

    Nowell, Nowell, Nowell, Nowell,
    born is the King of Israel.

6   Then let us all with one accord
    sing praises to our heavenly Lord,
    That hath made heaven and earth of nought,
    and with his blood mankind hath bought:

    Nowell, Nowell, Nowell, Nowell,
    born is the King of Israel.

Knitted Nativity – dotted around the church, who should be there?

Mary/Joseph/Shepherds/Kings/Animals.

As people are spotted, let them go and pick them up and return to form a mixed human/knitted tableau.

No Jesus, because he is born tonight.

We have another crib in this church; before we see it, let us sing 'While Shepherds Watched Their Flocks'.

While Shepherds Watched Their Flocks

1   While shepherds watched their flocks by night,
    all seated on the ground,
    the angel of the Lord came down,
    and glory shone around.

2   'Fear not,' said he (for mighty dread
    had seized their troubled mind);
    'glad tidings of great joy I bring
    to you and all mankind.

3   'To you in David's town this day
    is born of David's line
    a Saviour, who is Christ the Lord;
    and this shall be the sign:

4   'The heavenly babe you there shall find
    to human view displayed,
    all meanly wrapped in swathing bands,
    and in a manger laid.'

5   Thus spake the seraph; and forthwith
    appeared a shining throng
    of angels praising God, who thus
    addressed their joyful song;

6   'All glory be to God on high,
    and to the earth be peace;
    good will henceforth from heaven to men
    begin and never cease.'

The Voile is lifted from the Big Nativity.

Here we can see all those characters that we collected at the front of church.

Listen to the story from the Holy Bible:

A reading from the Gospel of Matthew:

Joseph lived in the town of Nazareth.
But one day he had to go all the way to Bethlehem with Mary
even though she was going to have a baby.

While they were in Bethlehem,
the baby was born – it was Mary's first little boy,
and she dressed him up in baby clothes
and made a bed for him in a stable
because there was no room left for them at the inn.

This is the word of the Lord.
Thanks be to God.

God, the powerful creator of the world, could have sent his Son in power and glory and forced us to be good; but God loves us, and wanted his Son to show us, not force us.

God sent Jesus in the world as a tiny, vulnerable baby; in an obscure corner of the world; so that the Saviour of the world would be one of us: tiny and vulnerable in this great big world.

It's very tempting to think only of the baby Jesus and to forget that this is not the end of the story, but only the beginning. The child born in a smelly, cold cave which sheltered animals would grow up, and the fabulous stories told of his birth would be mirrored by those wonderful things he did as an adult: to make the deaf hear, the blind see, the lame walk and to heal the sick; but none of that compares to the ultimate giving – the best present of all, the gift of our eternal life, won by the baby grown into the man, the man who offered himself on the cross.

So remember, don't keep the baby in the manger, don't cling on to the chocolate box image of the child, but allow the child to grow, and your faith will grow too – for the mature Jesus is the man who won us the ultimate freedom through the victory of the cross.

Christingles

This is a Christingle Service, which means I suppose that we should have some Christingles around here somewhere ... Oh yes, you have them in kit form! I hope no one has opened and eaten the sweets yet ...

Because this year I thought it would be a good idea for us to make our own, and you have the kit here.

Can anyone tell me what a Christingle is?

The Christingle was invented to explain symbolically God's goodness to the world. As this is quite a large crowd, I'm going to scale up my Christingle a little bit, so everyone can see. It features:

- An orange, which represents the world that God made.
- Four cocktail sticks, representing the four seasons, the four corners of the earth.
- Dried fruit and sweets representing God's gifts to the world.
- A red ribbon tied around the orange, representing the blood of Christ.
- A lighted candle representing Jesus Christ, shining in the world today.

Christingles not only signify the goodness of God to us, but they can also be a focus for Christmas.

If you can, replace the sweeties on the Christingle tonight and place it alight on your Christmas table, so, as you gather as a family, you can be reminded of the place that Jesus Christ has among your festivities.

Say Grace before your meal, and thank God for bringing you together as a family. On the outside of the bag there is a special grace that you can say together when you have relit your Christingle.

When you have completed your Christingle, let us gather before the altar rail, where we will light them.

The children will sing the first verse of 'Away in a Manger' in the candlelight, and then for the next two verses we will all join in.

Light Christingles. [LIGHTS OUT.]

Away in a Manger

(In dark, children first verse; second and third verse, all.)

1   Away in a manger, no crib for a bed,
the little Lord Jesus laid down his sweet head;
the stars in the bright sky looked down where he lay,
the little Lord Jesus asleep on the hay.

2   The cattle are lowing, the baby awakes,
but little Lord Jesus no crying he makes.
I love thee, Lord Jesus! Look down from the sky,
and stay by my bedside till morning is nigh.

3   Be near me, Lord Jesus: I ask thee to stay
       close by me for ever, and love me, I pray.
       Bless all the dear children in thy tender care,
       and fit us for heaven, to live with thee there.

Now, tomorrow is the birthday of Jesus Christ, our Lord and Saviour, and all these candles make it look a bit like a birthday cake.

I don't know if we have [*year*] candles here, but we have quite a lot. What song do we sing at someone's birthday? Why don't we all sing 'Happy Birthday Dear Jesus' to remind ourselves of why we celebrate Christmas – the birthday of the most special man ever in the history of the world!

   Happy birthday to you,
   Happy birthday to you,
   Happy birthday dear Jesus,
   Happy birthday to you!

Blow candles out.

Blessing

May the humility of the shepherds,
   the faith of the wise men,
   the joy of the angels,
   and the peace of the Christ Child,
be God's gift to us and to all people this Christmas.
And the blessing of God almighty,
the ⁺Father, Son and Holy Spirit,
be upon you and remain with you, this night and always.

Amen.

Depart

Go in peace to love and serve the Lord.
Thanks be to God.

THE SEDER MEAL

This Seder liturgy is a complete, slightly Christianized version of the Jewish celebration at the heart of our own eucharistic tradition. A much simpler liturgy, especially suitable for younger participants, can be found in the excellent *Welcome to the Lord's Table* by Margaret Withers.[64]

Passover is the great Jewish feast of redemption and liberation, where the people of Israel recall their deliverance from slavery in Egypt, as told in the book of Exodus 12, as God 'passed over the houses of the children of Israel in Egypt'.[65]

Passover is also known as the Feast of Unleavened Bread, since in their haste to flee Egypt, 'the people carried off their dough, still unleavened'[66] (i.e. without yeast). The lamb offered at each paschal meal recalls the first Passover sacrifice, whose blood protected the Israelites from the avenging angel of God.[67]

Each year, this deliverance is recalled by each Jewish family in the ritual of the Seder or Passover Meal. Its connection with the Eucharist is immediately obvious, even though there is conflicting evidence as to whether the Last Supper was indeed a Passover Meal.[68]

Gathered around the table with his disciples, Jesus told them:

'I have longed to eat this Passover with you before I suffer; because, I tell you, I shall not eat it again until it is fulfilled in the kingdom of God.'

Then, taking a cup, he gave thanks and said, 'Take this and share it among you, because from now on, I tell you, I shall not drink wine until the kingdom of God comes.'

Then he took some bread, and when he had given thanks, broke it and gave it to them, saying, 'This is my body which will be given for you; do this as a memorial of me.' He did the same with the cup after supper, and said, 'This cup is the new covenant in my blood which will be poured out for you.'[69]

The Jewish tradition makes great emphasis on the whole family, with their active involvement and a dialogue between generations which is a key part of the remembering or *anamnesis*. For this reason, as an introduction to the Eucharist,

---

64 M. Withers (2006), *Welcome to the Lord's Table*. London: Barnabas.

65 Exodus 12.27.

66 Exodus 12.34.

67 Exodus 12.21–33.

68 The timing of the Gospel of John suggests that the Last Supper is the night before the Passover so that Jesus represents the Lamb of God sacrificed at the same time as the Passover Lambs, although the Synoptic Gospels specifically describe it as a Passover Meal (e.g. Matthew 26.19).

69 Luke 22.15–20.

perhaps as part of the Admission to Holy Communion process or as a part of the teaching of Holy Week, a Christianized version of the Seder can be introduced.

Shape of the Seder

The eating of the Seder Meal is always accompanied by commentary, prayers and blessings. It is strongly recommended that prior to the celebration the participants are encouraged to read and reflect on the Scripture account of this event which is found in Exodus 7—13.

The actual Seder is a complete meal with supper during the ritual. In the service which follows, this ritual can be followed by a shared meal. Like the Seder itself, it should be festive and joyous.

The table should be set as for a usual dinner, with wine glasses for all, including children.

Each plate should have small portions of the following:

Haroset	Combine: ½ cup chopped nuts, ½ cup diced apple, I tbsp. cinnamon, I tbsp. sugar, red wine as desired. This recipe can be increased to serve any number; it should serve four to six people.
Maror	A bitter herb such as the top of the horseradish root or parsley.
Egg	One slice of hard-boiled egg.
Matzos	Matzos can be bought from most supermarkets.
Salt water	A separate small dish next to the dinner plate.
Wine and a wine glass	The glasses should be empty before the beginning of the meal as the pouring is highly symbolic. It might be necessary to use a fruit juice to symbolize the wine.
Lamb	A plate with a small piece of lamb for each person. This can easily be done by cooking a few lamb chops and cutting them into a sufficient number of pieces. In one setting it was not possible to use actual meat and so we had a picture of a lamb bone.
Candles	
Napkin	

Roles in the Seder

The roles in the Seder Meal are family focused and therefore are listed below in gender-specific roles. They may of course be reversed or indeed undertaken by any adult.

Father	The leader of the Seder.
Mother	The commentator, teacher and explainer.
Youngest child	Traditionally the 'four questions' are posed by the youngest person, but it might be more educational if the questions were shared by the children present.

The Seder Liturgy

Introduction

Mother: The central theme of the Passover is redemption. For us, Passover means not only the physical exodus from Egypt, but our spiritual passing over from the bondage of sin as well. The aim of the Seder on this night of the Passover is to bring the events and miracles of the past deliverance from Egypt into the present, so that each of us gathered here feels as though we had personally come out of bondage. We are asked to bear witness to God's redeeming action in the past, to act in conformity with his will in the present and to renew our hope in further redemption.

Kadesh: Blessing of the Day

Father: We gather for this sacred celebration in the presence of loved ones and friends with the signs of festive rejoicing around us. Together with the whole house of Israel, both young and old are linking the past with future; we respond in faith to God's call to service; we gather here to observe the Passover, as it is written:

All: 'The feast of unleavened bread must be kept, because it was on that same day I brought your armies out of the land of Egypt. Keep that day from age to age ...' (Exodus 12.17)

The Lighting of the Candles

Mother: In praising God we say that all life is sacred. In kindling these festive lights, we are reminded of life's sanctity. With every holy candle we light, the world is brightened to a higher harmony. We praise you, O Lord our God, King of the Universe, who hallows our lives with commandments and bids us to light these festive holy lights. (*She lights the festive candles.*)

Kiddush: The First Cup

Mother: We have blessed this day in the 'Kadesh', and called to mind the holiness of this festival commanded by the Lord. The candles we have lit praise God for the holiness of all life.

Now let us prepare to drink the first, the Kiddush, or cup of sanctification. Traditionally, four times during the meal wine is taken, recalling the four terms in the Exodus story which describe God's action in rescuing the Israelites: 'I brought out ... I saved ... I delivered ... I redeemed.'

We bless the wine and every food which is eaten, and every action which takes place, as a gesture of thanksgiving to the Creator of all things. (*The Leader pours wine for all.*)

Father: Our history teaches us that in varied ways and in different words God gave promises of freedom to our people. With cups of wine we recall each one of them, as now the first:

All: 'I am the Lord, your God. I will free you from the burdens which the Egyptians lay on you.' (Exodus 6.6)

Father: (*All raise wine glasses.*) We raise the Kiddush cup, and proclaim the holiness of the Day of Deliverance.

All: Blessed are you, O Lord our God, King of the Universe, who has kept us in life, sustained us, and brought us to this session of joy! (*All drink the first cup.*)

Karpas: Rebirth and Renewal

Mother: In the springtime each year, the season of rebirth and renewal, we read from the Song of Songs. This poetry of nature and of love recalls for us the love between God and the people of Israel, and their covenant relationship. The parsley symbolizes the growth of springtime, and is a sign of hope and renewal.

Father: 'See, winter is past, the rains are over and gone. The flowers appear on the earth. The season of glad songs has come ...' (Song of Solomon 2.10–12) (*Each person takes some greens and dips them twice in salt water.*)

All: Blessed are you, O Lord our God, King of the Universe, Creator of the fruit of the earth! (*The greens are now eaten.*)

Yahatz: A Bond Formed by Sharing

Mother: The leader breaks the middle matzo on his plate, wraps the larger half in a cloth, and conceals it as the 'afikoman'. This matzo is later shared as the final food of the Seder, but now serves as a visible reminder of the hidden Messiah whose appearance is expectantly awaited.

Father: (*While breaking the middle matzo.*) This is the bread of affliction, the poor bread which our ancestors ate in the land of Egypt. Let all who are hungry come and eat. Let all who are in want share in the hope of Passover. As we celebrate here, we join with people everywhere. This year we celebrate here. Next year in the land of Israel. Now we are still enslaved. Next year may we all be free.

The first of the leader's three matzot is broken and distributed.

All: Blessed are you, O Lord our God, King of the Universe, who brings forth bread from the earth. We praise you, who hallows our lives with commandments, and have commanded us regarding the eating of matzo and maror.

Mother: Matzo bread is used to recall the fact that the dough used by the fleeing Israelites had no time to rise before the act of redemption.

Maror, the top of the horseradish root, symbolizes the bitterness of the past suffering of the Jews in Egypt.

Haroset is a mixture of apples, spices, wine and nuts, and symbolizes the mortar the Jews used in carrying out the Pharaoh's labour.

According to ancient custom, maror and haroset are eaten between two pieces of matzot. Break the piece of matzo on your plate in half, and place some maror and haroset between.

All: In each of these elements we see the symbols of our story: the matzo of freedom, the maror of slavery, the haroset of toil. For in the time of bondage there is hope of redemption, and in the time of freedom there is knowledge of servitude.

All eat the matzo, maror and haroset.

The Four Questions

Youngest: Why does this night differ from all other nights? On all other nights
present   we eat leavened bread; why on this night only matzo?

On all other nights we eat all kinds of herbs; why on this night only bitter herbs?

On all other nights we do not dip our herbs at all; why on this night must we dip them twice?

On all other nights we eat in an ordinary manner; why on this night do we dine with special ceremony?

Maggid: The Story

Father: There are many questions to answer. Now we begin to respond to them. Our history moves from slavery toward freedom.

All: We were slaves to Pharaoh in Egypt, and the Lord freed us with a mighty hand. Had the Lord not delivered us from Egypt, we, our children and children's children would still be enslaved.

Father: Therefore, even if all of us were wise, if all of us were a people of understanding, and learned in the law and the prophets, it would still be our obligation to retell the story of the Exodus from Egypt. Anyone who searches deeply into its meaning is considered praiseworthy.

All: Our redemption is not yet complete.

As the leader lifts the paschal lamb.

Father: What is the meaning of the pasch?

Mother: This pasch represents the paschal lamb which our ancestors sacri-
            ficed to the Lord in memory of the night on which the Holy One
            passed over the houses of our ancestors in Egypt. As it is written:
            'And when your children ask you, "What does this ritual mean?"
            you will tell them, "It is the sacrifice of the Passover in honor of
            Yahweh who passed over the houses of the sons and daughters of
            Israel in Egypt, but spared our houses!"' (Exodus 12.26–27)

The leader holds up the upper piece of unleavened bread.

Father: What is the meaning of the unleavened bread?

Mother: It is the bread of affliction, which our ancestors took with them out
            of Egypt. For, as it is written: 'They baked cakes with the dough
            which they had brought from Egypt, unleavened because they had
            been driven out of Egypt with no time for dallying, and had not
            provided themselves with food for the journey.' (Exodus 12.39)

The leader replaces the matzo, and holds up the bitter herbs.

Father: What is the meaning of the maror?

Mother: Maror means bitter herb, and symbolizes the bitterness of past suf-
            fering which our ancestors experienced in Egypt. As it is written,
            'The Egyptians forced the children of Israel into slavery, and made
            their lives unbearable with hard labour, work with clay and with
            brick, all kinds of work in the fields; they forced on them every kind
            of labour.' (Exodus 1.13–14)

*This part of the service ends with the prayers of thanksgiving to God through
chanting one of the Psalms of deliverance, and drinking the second cup of wine,
the cup of deliverance.*

All together recite Psalm 114.

Psalm 114: Hymn for the Passover

Alleluia!

When Israel came out of Egypt, the House of Jacob from a foreign nation Judah became his sanctuary and Israel his domain.

The sea fled at the sight, the Jordan stopped flowing, the mountains skipped like rams, and like lambs, the hills.

Sea, what makes you run away? Jordan, why stop flowing?

Why skip like rams, you mountains, why like lambs, you hills?

Quake, earth, at the coming of your Master, at the coming of the God of Jacob, who turns rock into pool flint into fountain.

Father:	With the second cup of wine, we recall the second promise of liberation.
All:	'I will deliver you.' (Exodus 6.6)
Father:	It is written: 'And on that day you shall explain to your children, "This is because of what the Lord did for me when I came out of Egypt."' It is not only our ancestors that the Lord redeemed, but he redeemed us as well along with them, and all generations to come.

The participants raise their cups and say:

All:	Therefore, we are bound to thank, praise, honour, bless and adore him who brought us forth from slavery to freedom, from sorrow to joy, from mourning to feasting, from bondage to redemption, from darkness to great light. We praise you, O God, King of the Universe, Creator of the fruit of the vine!

All drink the second cup. The symbolic meal is now served.

Mother:	The meal is customarily begun with hard-boiled eggs flavoured with salt water. The egg is symbolic of new growth, new hope, new life.

Each person dips a slice of egg in salt water and eats it.

Mother:	The meat is eaten according to the custom that: 'The flesh (of the lamb) is to be eaten, roasted over fire; it must be eaten with unleavened bread and bitter herbs.' (Exodus 12.8)

The server now gives each person a piece of lamb, which is eaten.

Mother: We believe that at this point in the Lord's Supper Jesus instituted the Eucharist. We read in Luke's Gospel: 'He took bread, and when he had given thanks, broke it and gave it to them saying, "This is my body, which will be given for you; do this as a memorial of me."' (Luke 22.19)

Father: As we now share the bread of the afikoman, let us realize that the fellowship which binds us together is the grace and peace we share as members of the Body of Christ.

All eat of the afikoman.

Mother: Luke's account continues: 'He did the same with the cup after supper, and said, "This cup is the New Covenant in my blood which will be poured out for you"' (Luke 22.20). Here we clearly see the connection between the cup of Jesus' New Covenant and our final cup of the Seder, the cup of redemption. (*Wine is poured for each person.*)

Father: Let us together take up our cups of wine, and recall the final promise:

All: As it is written: 'I will redeem you with an outstretched arm.' Praised are you, O Lord our God, King of the Universe, Creator of the fruit of the vine!

All drink the final cup of wine.

Gesture of Peace

Father: We have now celebrated our unity in this symbolic meal, in sharing this bread and this wine. We recall the words of the Lord Jesus at this point in the Last Supper: 'Peace I leave you, my own peace I give you, a peace the world cannot give ....'

           Let us now offer one another an appropriate sign of the peace we have experienced here as the company of believers gathered to celebrate these mysteries of our faith.

All exchange a sign of peace.

Father: Let us conclude our ritual by joining our hands and hearts in praying the words which Jesus offered to his Father for us on the night we recall here.

All: Holy Father, keep those you have given me true to your name, so that they may be one as we are one … I am not asking you to remove them from the world, but to protect them from the Evil One … Consecrate them in truth – your word is truth. As you sent me into the world, I have sent them into the world … May they all be one. Father, may they be one in us, as you are in me and I am in you, so that the world may believe it was you who sent me.

Pause for silent prayer.

Final Blessing

Father: Let us bless each other.

All: May the Lord bless us and keep us! May the Lord let his face shine upon us and be gracious to us! May the Lord look upon us kindly, and grant us peace! Amen! (Numbers 26.22–27)

BLESSÉD SORRY SERVICE

A service of reconciliation for children (preparing for admission to Holy Communion) and adults who mess up as well.

This liturgy was inspired by a service contained in the excellent *Welcome to the Lord's Table*[70] by Margaret Withers, which is specifically used to prepare children for admission to Holy Communion. Typically, Blesséd has taken this and moved into new sacramental territory and made the liturgy its own.

Children love to sing, and so for this act of reconciliation you have the option to use certain cheesy classics, but you can choose from any appropriate substitutes or take up our own well-loved rhymes adapted from *The Nursery Rhyme Mass*.

There is something vivid about the confession process when we see our written confessions destroyed permanently. The written makes our sin tangible, and its destruction shows us powerfully the power of Christ over sin. The core of this liturgy uses a special paper called 'flash paper' and is used by magicians: a

---

70 M. Withers (1999), *Welcome to the Lord's Table*. Oxford: BRF.

touch of flame and it rapidly distintegrates leaving no trace, and it cannot fail to impress. Flash paper is building-safe and can even be held as it burns, although some care is advised. A good source can be eBay or a local magic shop. We invite people to write their sins on a small piece of flash paper and then place them in a balti dish for burning. This is very dramatic: children simply love it.

Do not be tempted to repeat the trick with the flash paper, even though children will beg you to do so: you will diminish the impact of it the next time. Sacramental worship is all about awe and wonder – keep it that way.

Gathering

Hymn: 'Seek Ye First' or Gathering Rhyme from 'The Nursery Rhyme Mass' (adapted).
(*To the tune of 'Here We Go Round the Mulberry Bush'.*)

We gather round in this holy space,
holy Space, filled with grace.
We gather round in this holy space
to do what Jesus taught us.

We hear the stories of Jesus, our King,
eternal life, for us he'll win.
Confess our sin and pray with him
and do what Jesus taught us.

Introduction

In the name of the +Father, and of the Son, and of the Holy Spirit.

We come together today as friends to sort things out with God. As we continue our Christian journey, we become ever more aware of how we mess up our relationships with other people and with God. Every time we do something wrong, and it hurts or upsets others, it also changes our relationship with God.

We call that damage to our relationship with God 'sin'.

But Jesus makes it right with God for us: by freeing us from our sins through the power of the cross and the resurrection, so that we are able to approach God as his sons and daughters.

God knows everything that we have thought and said and done, even if we forget all those things. If we want to make things right, we need to remember some of them, so during this act of saying sorry to God we shall all be invited to write or draw our wrongdoings and those of the world on the special paper provided.

By dying for us on the cross, Jesus took away all our sins, our wrongdoings. To symbolize this, our sins will be destroyed in a special and magical way.

We are, of course, not the first people to mess up our lives and our relationship with God. Right back to the beginning of the Bible, we hear how people who have loved God and messed up, made mistakes and wrong decisions, and yet God still loves them, as he loves us. To help us, we are going to think about Jesus' friend, Peter.

Peter promised to follow Jesus, but he denied knowing him a few hours later. Peter was very sorry when he realized what he had done. After the resurrection, Jesus forgave Peter and he became the great apostle who travelled all over the known world to teach people the Good News.

First Reading (Mark 14.27–31a)

You can do this as a direct reading, an animation (see Chapter 3 on storytelling) or a clip from a film such as *The Miracle Maker*. The text below is drawn from *The Message*, a contemporary translation by Eugene Peterson.[71]

> Jesus told his disciples, 'You're all going to feel that your world is falling apart and that it's my fault. There's a Scripture that says,
>
> "I will strike the shepherd; the sheep will go helter-skelter." But after I am raised up, I will go ahead of you, leading the way to Galilee.'
>
> Peter blurted out, 'Even if everyone else is ashamed of you when things fall to pieces, I won't be.'
>
> Jesus said, 'Don't be so sure. Today, this very night in fact, before the rooster crows twice, you will deny me three times.'
>
> He blustered in protest, 'Even if I have to die with you, I will never deny you.' All the others said the same thing.

71 Eugene Peterson (2007), *The Message*. Colorado Springs: Navigator Press.

Prayer

Jesus, we want to be your friends but, like Peter, we make promises that we do not keep. We let you down by not loving God or other people. Help us to remember the things that we have done wrong that have hurt you and our friends, and to be sorry for them. Amen

Follow with any other petitions.

Second Reading (Based on Mark 14.26–31, 66–72)

Again, a straight reading, animation or film clip can illustrate this reading.

Jesus was taken to the high priest's house. Peter followed from a distance and went into the courtyard of the high priest's house. One of the high priest's servant women came by. She looked straight at him and said, 'You, too, were with Jesus of Nazareth.'

But he denied it. 'I don't know him. I don't understand what you are talking about,' he answered, and went out into the passage. Just then a cock crowed.

The servant woman saw him there and began to repeat to the bystanders, 'He is one of them!' But Peter denied it again.

A little while later, the bystanders accused Peter again, 'You can't deny that you are one of them, because you too are from Galilee.'

Then Peter said, 'I swear that I am telling the truth! May God punish me if I am not! I do not know the man you are talking about!'

Just then a cock crowed a second time.

Then Peter remembered how Jesus had said to him, 'This very night before the cock crows twice you will say three times that you don't know me.'

And Peter broke down and cried.

As quiet music is played, the priest invites the people to move to a quiet place to write or draw their sins or the sins of the world on pieces of flash paper. As each person finishes, they come to the front and place their paper in a balti dish.

Prayer – said together

> Dear Jesus,
> Like Peter, we have let you down by not loving you or other people.
> Like Peter, we are sorry.
> Please forgive us and make us your friends again.
> Amen

Absolution

> God of mercy and power, forgive our faults and give us your grace to walk
> with you today and every day, through Jesus Christ our Lord.
> **Amen.**

> God loves us so much that Jesus came to destroy our sins through the
> victory of the Cross. This is what he does to our sins …

A light is set to the 'sins' in the balti dish as our sins are forgiven.

Absolution Hymn

*Hymn: 'God Forgave My Sin in Jesus' Name' or Absolution Rhyme from 'The
Nursery Rhyme Mass'.*
(To the tune of 'If You're Happy and You Know It'.)

You're forgiven and you know it, so clap your hands.
You're forgiven and you know it, so clap your hands.
You're forgiven and you know, so you really ought to show it,
you're forgiven and you know it, so clap your hands.

Jesus loves you and you know it, so stamp your feet.
Jesus loves you and you know it, so stamp your feet.
Jesus loves you and you know it, so you really ought to show it,
Jesus loves you and you know it, so stamp your feet.

If you believe that God forgives you, say 'We do' **'We do'.**
If you believe that God forgives you, say 'We do' **'We do'.**
When you say that you are sorry, you no longer have to worry,
God takes away your sin, so say 'Amen'. **Amen!**

Third Reading (Mark 16.1, 5–7; John 21.15–17, 19b)

Again, a straight reading, animation or film clip can illustrate this reading.

First reader

> After the Sabbath, Mary Magdalene, Salome and Mary the mother of James brought spices to put on Jesus' body ... The women went into the tomb, and on the right side they saw a young man in a white robe sitting there. They were afraid.
>
> The man said, 'Don't be afraid! You are looking for Jesus from Nazareth, who was nailed to a cross. God has raised him to life, and he isn't here ... Now go and tell his disciples, and especially Peter, that he will go ahead of you to Galilee. You will see him there just as he told you.'

Second reader

> When Jesus and his disciples had finished eating, Jesus asked, 'Simon, son of John, do you love me more than the others do?'
>
> Simon Peter answered, 'Yes, Lord, you know I do!'
>
> 'Then feed my lambs,' Jesus said.
>
> Jesus asked a second time, 'Simon, son of John, do you love me?'
>
> Peter answered, 'Yes, Lord, you know I love you!'
>
> 'Then take care of my sheep,' Jesus told him.
>
> Jesus asked a third time, 'Simon, son of John, do you love me?'
>
> Peter was hurt because Jesus had asked him three times if he loved him. So he told Jesus, 'Lord, you know everything. You know I love you.'
>
> Jesus replied, 'Feed my sheep ...' Then he said to Peter, 'Follow me!'

Final Prayers

> Peter followed, and faithfully told others of what Jesus had done for him. The Church was founded upon St Peter, so let us pray ...
>
> Risen Christ, thank you for letting us meet you here today.
>
> **Thank you, Lord.**

As you forgave Peter, so do you forgive us. Thank you for letting us come to know your forgiveness. Lord, you know we love you.

Thank you Lord.

Thank you for calling us to follow you. Help us to choose to do right, rather than wrong.

Thank you Lord.

Now, just as for Peter, God has work for us to do.
Let us go out to love and serve the Lord.

In the name of Christ. Amen.

Hymn – 'We are Marching'

There is no better way to end a children's service than in the joyous procession around the church to this South African tune: the more convoluted the route out of the nave to the narthex the better!

1   We are marching in the light of God,
we are marching in the light of God,
we are marching in the light of God,
we are marching in the light of God.
We are marching, oh,
we are marching in the light of God.
We are marching, oh,
we are marching in the light of God.

2   We are living in the love of God,
we are living in the love of God,
we are living in the love of God,
we are living in the love of God.
We are living, oh,
we are living in the love of God.
We are living, oh,
we are living in the love of God.

3   We are moving in the power of God,
we are moving in the power of God,
we are moving in the power of God,

we are moving in the power of God.
We are moving, oh,
we are moving in the power of God.
We are moving, oh,
we are moving in the power of God.

Traditional South African tune, verse 1 translated by Anders Nyberg; verses 2 and 3 by
Andrew Maries.[72]

Simple Words of Reconciliation

Priest: Lord God, we have done things today that were wrong. Lord, we are
sorry.
All: **Lord, we are sorry.**

Priest: For the times we have been unkind to people by saying things or
fighting. Lord, we are sorry.
All: **Lord, we are sorry.**

Priest: For the times we have not helped people who have needed our help.
Lord, we are sorry.
All: **Lord, we are sorry.**

Priest: For the times we have wasted the good things you give to us. Lord,
we are sorry.
All: **Lord, we are sorry.**

Priest: For the times we have not forgiven people who have been unkind to
us. Lord, we are sorry.
All: **Lord, we are sorry.**

Priest: Thank you Lord, for forgiving us when we are sorry and letting us
be your friends again. **Amen.**

Stones Penitential Rite

A video of this liturgy can be found at: http://vimeo.com/10039119.

This liturgy works well in this form with teenagers, although I have used and extemporized the handling and cradling of stones with children as young as seven. Touch is an often underused sense in worship, and yet it speaks directly to many. The fascinating variety of stones says something about our uniqueness and the ability to build even a basic pile with them shows how something constructive can be made with our messy, irregular lives.

Around the nave there are random heaps of stones in cairns (piles).

> Sin separates. It separates us from God, it separates us as a community. The stones of unity which are built into a temple, a cairn of living stones are torn apart and scattered.
>
> Take from this cairn a stone to hold, to transfer your sin into ...
>
> Cradle it, and let its hard exterior take on the hardness of your heart.
>
> Your stone carries the marks of wind and water, of weather, of spade and drill. It has history. It has past: just like your life. You carry the scars of your experience, maybe outside, maybe within.
>
> You hold in your hand something unique, something special, something of which there is not another anywhere in the world. Just like you.
>
> In places where God is rarely heard, in the dark and dismal places, these stones are ready to cry out in praise of God. Shed onto this stone your hurt, your doubt, your fear, your insecurity, your reluctance to reach out to the God who reaches out to you.
>
> The Lord, who makes all things and draws in unity all things, will take this from you, and release you from your burden ...
>
> Holy God, Maker of us all.
> **Have mercy on us.**
>
> Jesus Christ, Servant of the poor.
> **Have mercy on us.**
>
> Holy Spirit, Breath of life.
> **Have mercy on us.**
>
> Let us in silence remember our own faults and failings ...

God takes our hardness of heart, and replaces it with a heart of flesh. Let us rebuild the temple of living stones, and renew this church, this place, this people with our resolution to be reconciled to the God who reaches out to us.

I confess to God and in the company of all God's people that my life and the life of the world are broken by my sin.

May God forgive you, Christ renew you, and the Spirit enable you to grow in love.

Amen.

We confess to God and in the company of all God's people that our lives and the life of the world are broken by our sin

May God forgive you, Christ renew you, and the Spirit enable you to grow in love.

Amen

Screen: 'You are forgiven.'

The Lord has put away your sin, and please, pray for me, a sinner as well. **Amen.**

Stones on the Red Carpet

Equipment: a strip of red carpet or cloth on the floor, reminiscent of a movie première. The carpet is littered with stones.

A red carpet is often rolled out for celebrities or royalty when they arrive at big parties or film premières. It is rich and luxurious, smooth and comfortable, and makes them feel special. Only important people get the red carpet treatment.

We want to create a smooth red carpet for Jesus to arrive completely into our hearts, but sometimes we put boulders and obstacles in the way. The ground can be rough, we create hills for Jesus to climb over, and potholes can get in the way. As you can see, this path is not at all smooth: it is blocked by the stones of the wrong that we have done.

Take a moment to look closely at this broken path, and think about how those stones represent things that stop Jesus from arriving completely in your heart. What spoils your relationship with God? Worries? Harsh words? Anger? Nastiness? Think about them and how we might want to clear those things out of our lives and make a clear path for Jesus.

When you are ready, slowly and quietly come and take one of the stones from the carpet, so that we clear the way for the Lord. If we ask for forgiveness, then God will help us clear this path right into your heart, and he will come in glory especially for you on his smooth, luxurious red carpet of honour.

[*The people come forward and remove the stones.*]

The way is clear. We invite God into our hearts. By clearing this path you have shown your trust in the Lord and your hope of forgiveness. Your faith in Christ has saved you. Your sins are forgiven.

Amen.

Jennifer Clarke[73]

HEALING

A Liturgy for the Healing of a Child

The liturgies for healing in *Common Worship* are, in my personal opinion, woefully inadequate for either adults or children: they do not convey much confidence in the power of God's ability to heal or to reconcile the sick person to a comfortable death. They are completely inappropriate for use with children. It is no wonder therefore that any pastoral priest will vary from the authorized text in order to best serve those to whom they minister.

When a child is ill, they need reassurance, support and love. The sacramental signs of the sacrament of healing are very visible and useful symbols of this.

The sacrament of healing used to be regarded as the final act in an individual's life – 'the last rites' – and consequently the Church has neglected the powerful action of God's healing throughout our lives.

Children often role-play with toys or dolls as a way of working out their fears and anxieties, and the process of caring for a teddy or doll who coincidentally has exactly the same problem as the child, and who receives care from the child, is therapeutic. It is also telling when the dolly receives ill treatment (repeated injections or other forms of pain) as a way of the child trying to express his or her

---

73 Adapted with permission from the author.

own experience of care. If the child is known to have a doll or teddy in this role, it might need to be involved in the anointing as well. Some might sniffily dismiss the need to lay hands or anoint an inanimate object, but to the child, this doll or teddy is an extension of themselves[74] and it might be appropriate to share this act of healing with them.[75]

There are times when children who are ill also need to be agents of healing themselves. When parents are anxious or afraid, the child might wish to lay hands upon his or her parents. Healing is sometimes a two-way process.

Introduction

I have come to see you today because you're not feeling so well. It's hard when you don't feel so good, so I've come to pray with you, and to put some special oil on your forehead and hands. It's nice oil and it will make you feel special and good. This oil was made special by our bishop just before Easter, and priests like me use it to help.

When we feel sad or unwell we want a hug to make us feel better – Jesus knew that, and in the Bible we hear how he touched people and they were made better. St James told us that if anyone is ill, the priest should come and pray over them and put the special oil on them (James 5.14–15).

So, let us pray that God will help you …

We are here in the name of the [+]Father, and of the Son, and of the Holy Spirit. **Amen.**

The Lord be with you.
And also with you.

---

74 Philip Pullman in *His Dark Materials* series speaks of 'daemons' – a kind of avatar or external manifestation of the soul in animal form and not to be confused with the malevolent or demonic. For children, the doll or teddy becomes their avatar, walking with them through the illness experience.

75 Many years ago I was hugely touched by the impact of a kindly old monk who always blessed the dolls brought up to the altar rail by children. I have always sought to do the same, and the effect it has is transformative: try it and see for yourself. If nuclear submarines and tanks, bicycles and pets can be blessed, then why not a much-loved dolly?

Prayers of Penitence

Let's make right our relationship with God.
Lord Jesus, you heal the sick:
Lord, have mercy.
Lord, have mercy.

Lord Jesus, you forgive sinners:
Christ, have mercy.
Christ, have mercy.

Lord Jesus, you give yourself to heal us and bring us strength:
Lord, have mercy.
Lord, have mercy.

> May almighty God, who wipes away every tear from your eye, who hugs
> you in love and forgiveness, take away all that has happened, for he loves
> you, and restores you, in the name of the +Father, and of the Son, and of the
> Holy Spirit. **Amen.**

Laying On of Hands

> Jesus laid his hands upon those who were ill. In quiet, I'm going to do what
> Jesus did and pray that, as Jesus is here with us now, he will join his hands
> with mine and help you feel better.

Hands are laid upon the head in silence.

Anointing

> This oil is, as I said before, holy oil: prayed over by our bishop and set apart
> especially for this task – to help you feel better. It's not a medicine, but it's a
> way of showing God's love to you at this time – a love that will heal, a love
> that will comfort you.

> I'm going to put the oil on your forehead, in the sign of the cross, just like at
> your baptism, and on the palms of your hands: it's messy, but then again so
> is life, and as you feel the cool oil on your skin, let the love of Jesus surround
> you, hug you and help you.

Dip thumb.	Through this holy anointing
Down forehead.	may the Lord in his love and mercy
Across forehead.	help you, with the grace of the Holy Spirit. Amen.
Dip thumb.	
Down hand 1.	May the Lord
Across hand 1.	who frees you from sin
Down hand 2.	save you
Across hand 2.	and raise you up. Amen.

Through this holy anointing, may the Lord in his love and mercy help you, with the grace of the Holy Spirit. **Amen**
May the Lord who frees you from sin, save you and raise you up. **Amen**

Let us pray.

Dear Lord, thank you for being with us now. Help N and all who are ill or worried at this time, and may they always know that you are very near for them. Amen.

Blessing

The Lord be with you.
And also with you.

May almighty God give you strength, give you renewed hope and give you comfort throughout life's great adventure; and the blessing of God almighty, ⁺Father, Son and Holy Spirit, be with you, this day and always. **Amen.**

DISASTER RESPONSORY

Used with children in response to the Haitian earthquake in January 2010, but it can be applied to any natural disaster.

Images used and taken from the Internet can be found in PowerPoint on the CD-ROM in the **resources** directory as Haiti Response.ppt or as a series of images for you to put together in your own presentation package.

As a series of images of the disaster is shown on the screen, a random pile of bricks is formed after every couple of verses. However, from verse 22, tea lights are added to the pile of bricks, so that the cairn of bricks becomes a monument to those affected by the tragedy.

Lamentations 3.1–9, 22–24, 31–33

1 I am one who has seen affliction
   under the rod of God's wrath;
2 he has driven and brought me
   into darkness without any light;
3 against me alone he turns his hand,
   again and again, all day long.

4 He has made my flesh and my skin waste away,
   and broken my bones;
5 he has besieged and enveloped me
   with bitterness and tribulation;
6 he has made me sit in darkness
   like the dead of long ago.

7 He has walled me about so that I cannot escape;
   he has put heavy chains on me;
8 though I call and cry for help,
   he shuts out my prayer;
9 he has blocked my ways with hewn stones,
   he has made my paths crooked.

22 The steadfast love of Yahweh never ceases,
   his mercies never come to an end;
23 they are new every morning;
   great is your faithfulness.
24 'Yahweh is my portion,' says my soul,
   'therefore I will hope in him.'

31 **For Yahweh will not**
    reject us forever.
32 **Although he causes grief, he will have compassion**
    according to the abundance of his steadfast love;
33 for he does not willingly afflict
    or grieve anyone.

NRSV, adapted

We pray for the people of _____, for those who have died, and those who are bereaved. We pray for those who seek to bring relief and aid.

We pray alongside the whole world in the words our Saviour taught us:

Our Father, who art in heaven,
hallowed be thy name.
Thy kingdom come,
thy will be done,
on earth as it is in heaven.
Give us this day our daily bread.
And forgive us our trespasses,
as we forgive those who trespass against us.
And lead us not into temptation;
but deliver us from evil.
For thine is the kingdom,
the power and the glory,
for ever and ever.
Amen.

We may stay a while in silence to make our own private prayers.

There is no formal ending to this liturgy, as the young people may wish to pause in vigil and prayer, drifting away as they wish. It is most effective if this prayer response takes place at the end of the evening.

ALT. WORSHIP

Candles

We all teach from an early age that playing with fire is dangerous. Indeed it is, and yet the use of candles in worship is ancient and deeply evocative. With proper, close supervision, even very small children can be drawn into a sense of awe and wonder in gazing at a flame: a flame which they have helped to create. A gentle hand over theirs can light it, or a taper, and together the warm glow of a candle may be lit in a special safe place.

   The lighting of a candle is, of course, only a starting point, for it enables you to draw a moment of reflection, an activity of separation from the rest of the world and an inner peace.

   Some children may be afraid of the dark, and it is this candlelight which dispels the darkness, and brings comfort and peace.

> The world can sometimes seem a dark and scary place, with all kinds of bad things happening: wars and unhappiness, people being nasty to each other in the playground and in the park. You know from the newspapers and the TV news how grown-ups can be horrible to each other, and it feels as if the shadows of all the bad stuff are gathering in and darkening the world.
>
> If you have ever been caught in a power cut, you might remember how a once familiar room plunged into darkness becomes unknown: scary.
>
> Your parents might dig into a drawer or under the stairs and pull out a candle to light, and to help them to see just a little bit. See how even just one candle spreads its light into the darkness, and how the scary dark flees from the good light. That warm glow from a candle spreads warmth and comfort.
>
> Jesus said that he was the light of the world, the light that shines in the darkness.
>
> I believe that we each have a candle of faith inside us, and all we have to do is to light our candles of faith from the one true Light of the world. (*Light everyone's candle.*) When everyone's candle is lit, we can see so much more, and there isn't anywhere dark and scary around us any more.
>
> If we each lit our candle of faith from Jesus, the Light of the world, then all the scary stuff would no longer be so scary.

As you gaze into your flame and watch the flickering, warm light, think of the happy things in your life – those things which bring you joy, and those things that you do which bring joy to others. Let us thank God for them and promise that, with our candles of faith lit, we can brighten up the dark, scary places of the world with our love and joy.

Firebox

Firebox was created as a set of resources for the Diocese of Portsmouth Youth Department as a set of boxes that youth leaders could just pick up and use with their young people. The boxes contained everything you needed. Blesséd was asked to contribute and therefore drew together these meditations known as 'Firebox'. It was based on our understanding of the fascination that some young people have with fire. The box contained stones, balti dishes, charcoal, incense, a bucket and the liturgies. They can be recorded onto an MP3 player for personal reflection or read aloud by the leader.

Love and Self-control – A Meditation

You will need stones and sponges and a large bucket of water.
You can play low background music on a loop. A good example would be 'Proost – Inner Journey' from the Labyrinth Instrumental CD.

Come into this holy place. Enter and relax. God is here. Make yourselves at home.

Love can be as soft as sponges, or feel as hard as stones. It can make us feel warm and enriched. It can frustrate us, especially when love is painful, when love is unreturned, or when the love someone has for us prevents us from following our own selfish desires: the parent who won't let us out all night is the one who loves us.

Pick up a stone. Cradle it in the palm of your hand. Feel its smoothness and its broken edges.

Examine it closely. It's been shaped by centuries of waves and weather, damaged by explosion, by digging and building. Yet here it is, in your hand, in this field. In this place. In your possession.

It has been shaped by experience, good and bad; just as we are shaped by our experiences of life, of love.

'I will take your heart of stone,' the prophet told the words of God to the people, 'and give you back a heart of flesh.'

Our experiences can make our hearts as cold as this stone, as tough as rock. Emotions can bounce off it and nothing can touch it.

Do we think this makes us strong? Do we think that by putting up a strong shield against people we'll save ourselves from being hurt?

Do you really want a heart of stone?

'I will take your heart of stone, and give you back a heart of flesh.'

As you cradle this stone in your hand, pass on to it all those feelings of hardness in your life: those times when you have rejected others, been indifferent to their needs, their suffering. Let your selfishness coat this stone.

Now gently drop it into the water, and let it sink. It takes away with it those feelings, its toughness absorbs the tough things in your life, and the stream of living water which Jesus speaks of washes those feelings away.

'I will take your heart of stone, and give you back a heart of flesh.'

A heart of flesh is a heart which beats to the rhythm of the world, a heart of flesh is one which is open to the needs of those it meets. A vulnerable heart is one that is open to the love of God.

Take up a sponge. It is soft and yielding, it is flexible, pliable, responsive. It moves with you, and it moves with life. It is a heart which is open for God.

'I will take your heart of stone, and give you back a heart of flesh.'

Let my prayers rise before you like incense – Psalm 141

You will need a balti dish with sand in it, charcoal and incense. Ensure that the balti dish is placed on a heatproof mat or board. It can get hot and burn the carpet underneath. Add incense to the charcoal.

In the beginning there was nothing. Naught. Zilch. Nada.

In the midst of the nothing there formed a breath. The breath of God was moving in the nothing, and it formed, shaped.

The breath spoke and there was shape, and form, and substance.

See how the incense hangs in this place. See how it forms and re-forms. Uncapturable, unmastered. Shape and form and yet so wonderfully complex that we cannot describe it fully.

That is God. Beyond shape, beyond describable form and, just like the scent of holiness that now hangs in this space, it penetrates all that it touches. When you leave this place, the smell will be absorbed into your clothes. Deep into the fabric of our lives. This incense weaves the power of God.

And what do you see in the ever-changing column of smoke? Look and you might see faces, animals, clouds and figures. As the dancing smoke takes shape, breaks and re-forms, so all of God's creation is brought to mind.

And further, deeper, you see something more. A shape which is God's plans for you. Just as this smoke rises into the air, so do your prayers, your wishes, your deepest desires.

'Let my prayers rise before you like incense,' writes the psalmist.

Let your prayers rise.

And as your prayers rise, become absorbed into this holy smoke, breathe deeply. Inhale the breath of life, the breath of creation. The breath which brought you into being.

And listen, listen to what God says to you. Feel, in your soul.

Breathe on me, breath of God.

Amen.

Mirrors

Take an A4-sized mirror, or a mirrored bathroom tile, and attach an icon so that when you draw close to the mirror, you can see both your own reflection and the image of the icon at the same time.

[*Image of mirror/ikon.*]

Suggested music: 'Sometimes You Can't Make It On Your Own' by U2, from the album *How to Dismantle an Atomic Bomb*.

Words are unnecessary. Reflect on Christ. You are made in his image.

Water

The pouring of cool, flowing water over the hand. The fountain in the park. The ripple of the stream. Place children in the proximity of water, and the senses are heightened.

Flow

Our lives flow ever onwards, just like this stream/fountain. The water flows in one direction around your hand and on and on, to the sea, to the clouds. Each drop of water is part of a whole, just as you are part of the world. To God, each drop is precious and unique, just as you are precious and unique, special and loved.

Feel the cool sensation of this flowing water on your hand, the feeling it makes. The cold and tingly feeling it gives.

We can't turn back the flow of our lives, we can't turn this water around or make it flow uphill, we can't put it back to the beginning easily. What happens in our lives flows onwards and forwards: move on, do not be anxious or sad about the past, enjoy the sensation of this present world and look to the future, to where your lives may flow in the years to come.

Amen.

Beach

Stand on the shoreline and allow the waves to lap over your bare feet.

The sand shifts between our toes as we let the waves play around our feet. Can you feel the tickly sensation as the tide makes the sand move?

Lots of things happen which make us feel as though the world is changing beneath our feet and we feel insecure and uncertain. The water washes some grains away. Good stuff, bad stuff – washed away. Gone with the tide.

But then a new wave approaches. New grains are washed in. New experiences. New ideas. Provided by God.

The sand comes and goes with the water. Never more than we can bear. God knows what we need and what we can accept. As the tide retreats, what is left under our feet is new sand. It is solid. A sure footing for us to walk, knowing that God has provided a safe foundation for us to continue our lives.

Walk away on the solid sands, or wade deeper into the lapping sea. Feel God at work as the water moves to and fro around your feet. The change that is happening all the time is in God's hands. It's all under control. Trust in God and know that he is always there with you.

Lorraine Rundell[76]

Multisensory Experiences

Bittersweet

A video of this ritual can be found at http://www.vimeo.com/6206010.
Equipment: balti dishes, laminated signs (see below), spoons, honey, lemons.

1 min. 45 sec. introduction:

Life is complex and hard. Life is challenging and not without its fair share of pain. The preacher on TV who offers you untold riches, health, wealth, healing and joy has clearly never read the book of Job.

Life is beautiful and delicate. Life is filled with joy and laughter. The glass which was created by God is always at least half-full, beyond half-full, and closer to full to overflowing.

To see life as either one or the other is to miss the point of life in all its rollercoaster of variety. We learn in life to take the bitter and the sweet.

Around this sacred space are a number of stations, where you may taste in the lemon the bitterness of life, where you can offer to God in penitence those difficult, trying, hard things in your life. You may also taste a spoonful of honey – to 'taste and see that the Lord is good' as the Psalmist said, and to give thanks to God for his many, many blessings.

Without one, there is no other. Without both, life is meaningless. Offer them both to God in penitence and faith, and let us now be reconciled to God.

Stations: Four or six stations with a balti dish of lemons (and a bin and wipes) and a dish of honey with small spoons to taste a lemon and a spoon of honey.

76 Used with the permission of the author.

Each station has a text by it:

> Taste the bitterness of life.
> Without this, the sweet,
> good times are nothing.
>
> Give to God the pain, the
> sadness and the hurt.
>
> Taste and see that the Lord is good.
> ---
> Taste the sweetness of life.
> Without this, the bitter,
> ugly, hard times become
> everything.
>
> Give thanks to God for the joy,
> the pleasure and the laughs.
>
> Taste and see that the Lord is good.
> ---
> In happy moments, praise God.
> In difficult moments, seek God.
> In quiet moments, worship God.
> In painful moments, trust God.
> In every moment, thank God.

Absolution

Screen: 'You are forgiven'

Our Lord Jesus Christ, who has left power to his Church to absolve all sinners who truly repent and believe in him, of his great mercy forgive you all your offences; and by his authority committed to me, I absolve you from all your sins: ⁺In the Name of the Father, and of the Son, and of the Holy Spirit.

The Lord has put away all your sins, and of your charity, pray for me, a sinner also.
Amen.